"IT IS MY LAND, MY HO[...]
LAND, TO WHICH I NO[...]
LOWED TO RETURN. I W[...]
LAST DAYS THERE, AND BE BURIED AMONG
THOSE MOUNTAINS. IF THIS COULD BE I
MIGHT DIE IN PEACE, FEELING THAT MY
PEOPLE, PLACED IN THEIR NATIVE HOMES,
WOULD INCREASE IN NUMBERS, RATHER
THAN DIMINISH AS AT PRESENT, AND THAT
OUR NAME WOULD NOT BECOME EXTINCT."

—Geronimo

FREDERICK TURNER is the author of seven works of nonfiction and editor of three others. His books include *Beyond Geography: The Western Spirit against the Wilderness; Rediscovering America: John Muir in His Time and Ours;* and *A Border of Blue: Along the Gulf of Mexico from the Keys to the Yucatán.* He is the editor of the *Viking Portable North American Indian Reader.* His most recent book is *1946: When the Boys Came Back.*

Geronimo (1829–1909). From a photograph by A. Frank Randall, 1886. (*COURTESY OF THE ARIZONA HISTORICAL SOCIETY, TUCSON*)

GERONIMO

HIS OWN STORY

As Told to S. M. Barrett

Newly Revised and Edited,
with an Introduction and Notes by
Frederick Turner

A MERIDIAN BOOK

MERIDIAN
Published by the Penguin Group
Penguin Group (USA) Inc., 375 Hudson Street, New York, New York 10014, U.S.A.
Penguin Group (Canada), 90 Eglinton Avenue East, Suite 700, Toronto, Ontario,
Canada M4P 2Y3 (a division of Pearson Penguin Canada Inc.)
Penguin Books Ltd., 80 Strand, London WC2R 0RL, England
Penguin Ireland, 25 St. Stephen's Green, Dublin 2, Ireland (a division of Penguin Books Ltd.)
Penguin Group (Australia), 250 Camberwell Road, Camberwell, Victoria 3124, Australia
(a division of Pearson Australia Group Pty. Ltd.)
Penguin Books India Pvt. Ltd., 11 Community Centre, Panchsheel Park,
New Delhi – 110 017, India
Penguin Group (NZ), 67 Apollo Drive, Rosedale, North Shore 0632, New Zealand
(a division of Pearson New Zealand Ltd.)
Penguin Books (South Africa) (Pty.) Ltd., 24 Sturdee Avenue, Rosebank,
Johannesburg 2196, South Africa

Penguin Books Ltd., Registered Offices: 80 Strand, London WC2R 0RL, England

Published by Meridian, an imprint of Dutton Signet, a division of Penguin Books USA Inc.
Previously published in a Dutton edition.

First Meridian Printing (Newly Revised and Edited Edition), March 1996
30 29 28 27 26 25 24

Introduction and Notes copyright © Frederick Turner, 1970, 1996
The map "Apache Country 1865-1886" is reprinted with permission of Charles Scribner's Sons, from
Atlas of American History, Second Revised Edition. Copyright © 1984 Charles Scribner's Sons.
All rights reserved

REGISTERED TRADEMARK—MARCA REGISTRADA

LIBRARY OF CONGRESS CATALOGING-IN-PUBLICATION DATA
Geronimo, 1829–1909.
[Geronimo's story of his life.]
Geronimo : his own story / as told to S. M. Barrett.—Newly rev. and edited,
with an introd. and notes / by Frederick Turner.
p. cm.
Originally published: Geronimo's story of his life. New York: Duffield, 1906.
ISBN 978-0-452-01155-7
1. Geronimo, 1829–1909. 2. Apache Indians—Biography. 3. Apache Indians—Kings and rulers.
4. Apache Indians—Wars. I. Barrett, S. M. (Stephen Melvil). II. Turner, Frederick W. III. Title.
E99.A6G3 1996
973.8'092—dc20
[B]
95-33574
CIP

Printed in the United States of America
Set in Bembo
Designed by Jesse Cohen

BOOKS ARE AVAILABLE AT QUANTITY DISCOUNTS WHEN USED TO PROMOTE PRODUCTS OR SERVICES.
FOR INFORMATION PLEASE WRITE TO PREMIUM MARKETING DIVISION, PENGUIN GROUP (USA) INC., 375
HUDSON STREET, NEW YORK, NEW YORK 10014.

Dedicatory

Because he has given me permission to tell my story; because he has read that story and knows I try to speak the truth; because I believe that he is fair-minded and will cause my people to receive justice in the future; and because he is chief of a great people, I dedicate this story of my life to Theodore Roosevelt, President of the United States.

GERONIMO

Contents

Contents

PART III The White Men

PART IV The Old and the New

Illustrations

GERONIMO
HIS OWN STORY

Preface

The initial idea of the compilation of this work was to give the reading public an authentic record of the private life of the Apache Indians, and to extend to Geronimo as a prisoner of war the courtesy due any captive, *i.e.*, the right to state the causes which impelled him in his opposition to our civilization and laws.

If the Indians' cause has been properly presented, the captives' defense clearly stated, and the general store of information regarding vanishing types increased, I shall be satisfied.

I desire to acknowledge valuable suggestions from Major Charles Taylor, Fort Sill, Oklahoma; Dr. J. M. Greenwood, Kansas City, Missouri; and President David R. Boyd, of the University of Oklahoma.

I especially desire in this connection to say that without the kindly advice and assistance of President Theodore Roosevelt this book could not have been written.

Respectfully,
S. M. BARRETT.

LAWTON, OKLAHOMA.
August 14, 1906.

Introduction

I

In the midst of what is currently called the Gila National Forest in New Mexico, the Middle Fork of the Gila River rushes down out of the Mogollon Mountains. Except during the high tide of spring's runoff, it is a clear stream and, though not a wide one, it has through millennia cut a deep canyon. In places the canyon slopes are covered from summit to streamside with jumbled talus that makes walking slow and laborious. Where the soil is visible it is the color of baker's chocolate, with here and there patches that look like ancient blood. All around tower the well-wooded slopes of the Mogollons with their heavy ponderosas, their junipers, and groves of aspen. The light and air here are mercilessly clear, the shadows deep and razor-edged, so that the whole landscape has an almost photo-realist quality.

This was once the heart of Chiricahua country, and historians of that division of the Apaches now believe Geronimo was born somewhere on the Middle Fork, perhaps in 1823. Readers of the narrative that follows here will quickly find, however, that Geronimo himself said he was born over in Arizona in 1829. Angie Debo, Geronimo's most thorough biographer, suggests the birthplace might be near what is now

Clifton, Arizona, though she is willing to concede that the Middle Fork of the Gila is also a possibility. This is not, as she rightly says, a merely academic matter even if at this point it can never be definitely settled, for a Chiricahua's specific birthplace was a sacred spot to the child and his or her parents, and it was customary for the parents to bring the child back to it at some point and roll him on the ground in the four directions. Even when grown, an Apache would return to the spot and roll to the cardinal points, to maintain and revivify connection with the sources of his being. But historians incline to the New Mexican site for Geronimo's birthplace because so many other tribal sources have insisted on it. Asa Daklugie, who translated for Geronimo in the making of the autobiography and who was his second cousin, was emphatic on this point and so were many of the Chiricahuas whom historian Eve Ball interviewed on the Mescalero Reservation.

The discrepancy points up an important fact that must be borne in mind when reading this book, for we are dealing here with a preliterate and essentially prewhite narrative in which the dates and places on which white historiography depends are unimportant. To Geronimo the location of his birthplace was crucial; what the whites eventually came to call it was not. When he was born there wasn't any such place as "Arizona," or "New Mexico," either. This was instead Apache territory to which the Mexicans had advanced some weak claims, but the Apaches honored neither the Mexicans nor their claims. Instead, they regarded them as a treacherous, untrustworthy people who often got the Apaches drunk on mescal and then attacked them. The few and scattered Mexican settlements in northern Chihuahua and Sonora were mainly considered legitimate targets for Apache raiders and warriors, stable sources of meat, guns, ammunition, blankets, and alcohol. These, Geronimo insists, were the only things Mexicans were really good for.

II

In fact, by the time of Geronimo's birth the energy of Spain's colonizing industry had long since been dissipated and the villages of northern Chihuahua and Sonora had become more outposts than outposts of progress. But to begin with, of course, it had been the Spanish who had brought the full force of Western Civilization to the New World, and when Columbus dropped anchor in the Antilles that autumn day in 1492, the lives of the Chiricahuas and all the other tribes had entered a fateful new phase—Arawaks, Aztecs, Pamlicos, Wampanoags, Mohawks, Shawnees, Lakotas, Bannocks, Yokuts. . . .

If Columbus was the essential mind of the West, gathering and synthesizing centuries of accumulated knowledge of navigation and exploration, then Cortés was its active arm, putting all that knowledge to practical use. On Good Friday 1519, he made his landfall near what is now Vera Cruz, burned his ships behind him, and then began on the long march toward the conquest of the Americas. In subsequently defeating the vastly superior forces of the Aztecs and then sacking their powerful empire, Cortés initiated a pattern repeated everywhere in the New World, for he succeeded partly by exploiting intertribal antagonisms; partly through the incidental spread of communicable diseases against which the natives were defenseless; and partly because of the imponderable advantages conferred by the possession of the horse and the gun.

But there was something else that the Spanish packed

along with them into Mexico, into Peru where they humbled the haughty Incas, and northward into the superb aridity of the American Southwest where they sought (vainly) other empires to conquer. This was no mightier cannon, no indefatigable charger capable of drinking the wind. Rather it was a hemispheric habit of mind, a fierce and unappeasable hunger for more: more gold, more precious gems, more slaves, more converts, spices, tribute, and more land—especially more land. The Aztecs and the Incas themselves had thought big, had built empires and enslaved their near neighbors, but, after all, their visions proved puny in comparison with those of the Spanish and other colonizing powers of the Old World, the Portuguese, the British, and the French. And in the perspective of history this difference between natives and newcomers was critical. Time and again native leaders from Moctezuma to Powhatan to Red Cloud thought they could buy off the newcomers with gold or land cessions or treaties, only to discover too late that it wasn't possible to buy white men off: they were in this peculiar way incorruptible. At the same time, the tribes bought the whites' promises that certain lands would be theirs forever—the Iroquois Confederacy lands, the whole of the trans-Mississippi West, the Black Hills, Indian Territory—only to learn too late that the whites wanted *all* of it, every acre. So, the Iroquois lands became New York State, the trans-Mississippi West became the appointed goal of Manifest Destiny, the Black Hills became South Dakota, and Indian Territory, Oklahoma. It was not, as so often charged, that the natives were stupid in their dealings with the whites, capable of selling huge tracts of land for a few dollars and a mirror. But there is no doubt they never really understood them.

Native Americans never understood that unappeasable hunger for more that was the subtext of every one of the treaties, and the reason they didn't was precisely because they themselves remained captive to those locales where, so they believed, the Great Spirit had so purposefully placed them. Here was the traditional Chiricahua method for the disposal of afterbirth: the mother wrapped it in the piece of cloth or blanket on which she had knelt in labor and placed it in the branches of a nearby fruit-bearing bush or tree. "May the child live," she chanted to the tree, "to grow up and see you bear fruit many times." Thus the site was doubly sacred and the landscapes of all the tribes were peppered with sacred spots, creating for them homelands whose hold on the people was multiple, mystical, and unbreakable. This captivity was expressed in rituals like the Chiricahua ones of birth; in elaborate, prolonged ceremonies like the Navajo Mountain Chant; in legends and myths that were always rooted in particular locales. In all of these and in the round of daily life the discrete phenomena of place spoke to the people, reminding them of who they were and from whence they had sprung. Trees, which to the civilizing whites seemed nuisances and gloomy reminders of a wilderness continent, had voices for the natives. Rocks that merely broke the boards and blades of white farmers' plows were often for the tribes sources of Power.

The Iroquois, for instance, told of a young hunter's accidental encounter with the last of the Stone Giants, whose very glance could kill. When the young man sought shelter in a cave that happened to be the refuge of Ga-nus-quah, the monster spared his life because he had come in peace. But Ga-nus-quah did so on condition: that the young man dedicate his life to honoring the trees and the animals of the forest. Go, Ga-nus-quah told him at last, and teach the human beings the language of the forest and about the brotherhood of all things. The same people told of a Seneca orphan boy who was bird-hunting in the forest when he happened into a clearing where there sat a high, smooth stone with a flat top. The boy clambered up to this natural seat and was sitting there making repairs on an arrow, when the stone spoke, asking if he would like to hear some stories. So began a long saga, continued over many days and that eventually drew the entire village out to the clearing to listen. The stories the stone told were of the long ago, and in hearing them the people came to understand who they were and why they had been placed here. Thereafter, they called themselves the People of the Stone.

With such sources of attachment to place, how could the Iroquois (the closest to imperialists North America ever fostered) have even conceptualized the conquest of far-off peoples like the Blackfeet or the Chiricahuas? What out on the Great Plains or in the Southwest would have spoken to them like the basswood tree from which they carved the masks of Ga-nus-quah or the granite boulders of the forest clearings? How could their gods speak to them out of alien landscapes, and where would they look to find the sources of *orenda*, or Power?

This was not a problem for the whites. For many centuries their religion had been strenuously weaning them from intimate attachment to any locales, encouraging them instead to regard themselves as but sojourners on the long road that led to that point at which this chimerical earth would disappear and they would shuck it off for Heaven. They were similarly encouraged to regard as devilish any religious practices founded on natural phenomena. Thus in a real sense the drama of the conquest of the Americas was prefigured for them in the Old Testament, where they read of the wandering Israelites' defeat of the nature-worshipping tribes who opposed them with their false gods whose feet were both of and in the clay of the ancient Near East.

That drama seemed the more obvious and clearly defined once the English established a beachhead on the Outer Banks and the Northeast. Despite their ruthless subjugation of the tribes on the islands of the Caribbean and then in Mexico and portions of South America, the Spanish did have a Latin-Catholic kind of tolerance for heathenism and, taking the long view, believed that in time truth would triumph over error. They allowed the persistence therefore of certain aboriginal practices within the True Faith. Not so with their Protestant adversaries in North America, for whom everything had to go and no last vestiges of aboriginal ways could be suffered to endure. And as Latin-Catholic tolerance allowed some remnant tribal units to remain and even looked the other way when some Spanish began to intermarry with Indians, in North America, Protestant intolerance mowed down the tribes and their once-sacred landscapes with the indiscriminate efficiency of clear-cutting loggers. The Spanish built their cathedral directly atop the ruins of the great temple of Tenochtitlán, but behind its altar the native gods still dispensed a shadowy power to the increasingly mixed-blood parishioners. There weren't any temples in North America, only the lands themselves, and the whites transformed these as quickly and thoroughly as they were able.

Until the end of the 1820s, the process was piecemeal and poorly articulated. But with the election of Andrew Jackson matters moved into a higher gear, for if Columbus had been the mind of the West and Cortés its arm, in North America Andrew Jackson was both mind and muscle united into the essential personality of the Pioneer. He was shrewd, practical, and courageous. He also hated Indians and had no interest in the land except as it could be turned to what were then styled the "arts of civilization," i.e., agriculture and industry. If this was a somewhat diminished definition of what civilization amounted to, it was at least serviceable. The Indian Removal Act that Jackson signed in 1830 was a truly representative piece of legislation—representative in the sense that it expressed the wishes of all white Americans who wanted to see their country move forward. Now progress, great as it had undoubtedly been, would seem faltering and timid by comparison to what was begun in 1830. All the Indians, those visible reminders of the past and bars to future progress, were to be removed west of the Mississippi River, where their wasteful nomadic habits would trouble only a few. No matter that certain tribes like the Cherokees had ably learned to walk the white man's road, had established schools, libraries, mills, churches, and shops in the Old Southwest. Within five years after Removal became official policy, the Cherokees were started on the long walk westward, leaving behind them their farms, stock, and mills to be taken over by the white dispossessors. They joined the Ottawas, Potawatomis, Wyandots, Kickapoos, Winnebagos, Delawares, Peorias, and Miamis. In Illinois, an old war chief of the Sac and Fox tribe hoped for an alliance between his people and the Winnebago and Potawatomi tribes that would succeed in breaking the wave of the future. Black Hawk was even deluded enough to imagine that the British would help, but *that* tribe had already been crushed by the American juggernaut and wanted no part of further schemes to oppose it. The result was a hopeless, pathetic fifteen-week war during which various heroes of white history—Abraham Lincoln, Jefferson Davis, Zachary Taylor, and Winfield Scott (he would later tread Cortés's road to Mexico City)—collaborated to crush the rebellion. Black Hawk and his confederate chiefs were summoned to Washington, where the Great Father told them to be good and go west.

There can be few clearer examples of white America's lack of relationship to the natural world than this policy of removal, for it was done in callous disregard of the consequences of dumping thousands of alien Indians into an area the natural resources of which had provided abundant support for the tribes living there. But these resources were not, as both reds and whites were to discover, inexhaustible, and the forced arrival of these displaced tribes produced immediate strains and upsets in the ecology that resulted in the warfare for which the Plains Indians became famous. Both humankind's understanding of its proper relationship to the earth and the loss of that understanding—the Garden of Eden myth— were reenacted in the mopping-up operations carried on from 1850 to 1890. This blood-soaked, disease-ridden tragedy was played out against the backdrop of a region so overpoweringly beautiful in both its harsh and lush extremes as to dwarf into mockery the relentless antics of the dispossessors. Treaties were signed—and broken—for "as long as the grass shall grow," and Indians swept into battles of foregone conclusions, singing that it was a good day to die, for nothing lives long, "only the earth and the grass." But even the native grasses were being exterminated as the West was made over into farms and ranches: 142 million acres of the continent's heartland that for millennia had been thronged with big bluestem, blazing star, wild indigo, black Sampson, butterfly milkweed, compass plant, prairie smoke, Scribner's panicum, golden alexander, shooting star, and prairie dock.

When the Lakotas in Minnesota rose up and killed as many as five hundred whites in 1862, leaving a region fifty miles by two hundred miles barren of inhabitants, the nation was shocked. Then the whites gathered themselves for a final assault. Heroes of the Civil War were elevated to positions of central command of the operations. One of them, William Tecumseh Sherman (the middle name would become grimly ironic in the next few decades), responded in approved military fashion to the depredations of the Lakotas. "We must act with vindictive earnestness against the Sioux," he said, "even to their extermination, men, women, and children. Nothing else will reach the root of this case." And to his brother John, United States Senator from Ohio, he wrote a contemplated assessment of the situation: "The more we can kill this year, the less will have to be killed the next war, for the more I see of these Indians the more convinced I am that all have to be killed or maintained as a species of pauper." Rarely has history afforded us an example of such effective execution of orders. Another hero, Philip Sheridan, is credited by Ralph K. Andrist with the original remark about "good Indians." At Fort Cobb, Indian Territory, a Comanche named Turtle Dove introduced himself to the general with the humble self-attribution that he was a "good Indian." "The only good Indians I know," the general returned, "are dead." Such remarks make clearer than reams of official documents what the real operating procedure was to be in the Plains campaigns: it was to be extermination, pure and simple. Nothing—not the destruction of men, women, children, ponies, bison, grass, the very land itself—was permitted to arrest the machinelike operation, and if some of the village cleanups (like that at Sand Creek in 1864) were pretty bloody, these were but the inevitable hardships of making the continent. The whites proved better able to bear them than the tribes.

There were, of course, atrocities on both sides during the Long Death, but as Andrist observes, the supposed gap between the savage and the civilized often narrowed so that one was indistinguishable from the other. If anything, the whites sometimes showed greater ingenuity in their killing and mutilating than the Indians for whom such activities were presumed to be second nature. Few Indians, for example, would have been capable of the antics of certain white residents of Montana who cut off the heads of slain Indians, pickled the ears in whiskey, boiled the skin from the skulls, and then inscribed the bleached bones with such witticisms as "I am on the reservation at last."

So it went, onward to its relentless conclusion, through dozens of random massacres like the Fetterman Fight, where the Lakotas rubbed out eighty whites in forty-five minutes; the battle of the Washita, where Custer earned the praise of whites and the undying enmity of reds by surprising Black Kettle's friendly camp, killing perhaps as many as a hundred Indians and 875 ponies; and the celebrated Battle of the Little Big Horn, where the massed forces of Lakotas and Cheyennes overran Custer and his portion of the Seventh Cavalry. But the next year, 1877, it was really all over on the Plains. Andrist writes that as

1877 ended, in all the Great Plains, from Canada south, there was no longer a free tribe or a "wild" Indian. It had not taken long; in 1840 the boundary of the permanent Indian Country had been completed and the Great Plains were to belong forever to the Indians. A mere thirty-seven years later every solemn promise had been broken and no bit of ground large enough to be buried in remained to any Indian that could not—and probably would—be arbitrarily taken from him without warning.

By 1883 the destruction of the once limitless herds of bison that had roamed the Plains was virtually complete. It had become an article of faith with Sherman and Sheridan that the quickest way to insure the destruction of the Indians was to destroy their sources of livelihood. As part of such a plan, the army attempted the large-scale destruction of the forage for both the bison and the Indian ponies. Then in 1871 a new technological wrinkle, one of the many inventions that transformed the nineteenth century into the preeminent century of progress, made the wholesale slaughter of bison even more attractive than before: the perfection of a process whereby excellent leather could be fashioned from tanned buffalo hide. It was the bison, as the Cheyenne George Bent recalled, and the horse that made his people (and the other Plains tribes) "one of the proudest and most independent men that ever lived." Now that way of life—its humans, its animals, its grasses—was gone, and it remained only for the whites to tie up the loose ends in California to complete the process. In 1848, when gold was discovered in that area and it was annexed as a state, there were approximately one hundred thousand Indians there; by 1859, that figure had been reduced to about thirty thousand; and by the turn of the century there were only fifteen thousand of the race once described by a devotee of the American way as a "set of miserable, dirty, lousy, blanketed, thieving, lying, sneaking, murdering, graceless, faithless, gut-eating skunks as the Lord ever permitted to infect the earth, and whose immediate and final extermination all men, except Indian agents and traders, should pray for." To an appalling extent the prayers were answered.

III

A small, almost incidental, step in this march of progress was the subjugation, deportation, and drastic reduction of the Apache tribes of the Southwest. It was late and it was limited to the present states of Arizona and New Mexico with tedious campaigns into Old Mexico, but it was bloody, and it produced its fair share of heroes, villains, and fools.

It may have been Coronado's blundering and fruitless expedition that produced the first contact between whites and Apaches, but the reference of Pedro Castañeda de Najera, the expedition's official chronicler, to some nomadic desert people is both obscure and passing. By the beginning of the seventeenth century, however, the Apaches had been identified by the Spanish as threats to the settlement of northernmost New Spain and had already assumed the guise they would wear in Spanish and American accounts forever after: savages. "They hurl themselves at danger," wrote a Spanish missionary, "like a people who know no God nor that there is any hell."

Their prehistory is all but unknown, though from linguistic analysis it is believed they migrated from Alaska into the Southwest along with other Athapaskan peoples. Just when they reached their final destination remains an open and probably unanswerable question; the mid-fourteenth century has been proposed. For they were nomads who traveled far and traveled light, and when one visits a museum with Native American exhibits one finds the Apaches almost as invisible now as the Spanish and then the Americans did when they sought to track them: a few cane arrows maybe; a quirt; the tatter of a woven basket. Next to the magnificent Redware pottery of the Anasazis, it isn't much to go on. Even their name, *Apache*, and their tribal divisions are subjects of scholarly debate, since by the time ethnologists began systematic work among them the tribal cultures had been severely damaged by military defeat, deportation, and disease, and much consequently had been forgotten. Morris Opler and Grenville Goodwin in the 1930s tried to establish some large, general outlines of prereservation life, and Opler concluded there once had been four main Apache tribes—the Mescaleros, Lipans, Jicarillas, and Chiricahuas—within which there were numerous bands. From what he could deduce about the Chiricahuas, they had been further subdivided into three divisions, the southernmost of which had ranged through the Mexican states of Sonora and Chihuahua, until toward the middle of the nineteenth century the pressure of Mexican settlement pushed them northward into southwestern New Mexico and southeastern Arizona. Geronimo was born into this division and identified himself as a Bedonkohe, evidently a band.

When he dictated his life story to S. M. Barrett through his kinsman Daklugie, Geronimo had his reasons for seeking to convey the impression that the Chiricahuas had become the fierce warriors they were because of the slave-hunting expeditions of the Mexicans. There is some truth to this, or at least this much: the Mexicans did make slave raids on the Chiricahuas and eventually found that people so hostile and resourceful an enemy that they began offering a bounty on Apache scalps. But the likelihood is strong that the Chiricahuas were skilled in the arts of warfare by the time they reached Mexico. They hunted, to be sure, with clubs, spears, bows, and arrows (though somewhere along the way down from Alaska they had developed a taboo against fishing), and they may have raised a few melons and squashes on streamside plots in the valleys. But by the time we have any accounts of them they seem far too skilled in war to have been simply embattled hunters and gatherers, and they had the nomad-warrior's characteristic contempt for settled peoples. Indeed, a careful reading of Geronimo's account of Chiricahua culture suggests that the periodic raid of the settlements was regarded as a legitimate economic activity, something a band might undertake when supplies of meat or ammunition or guns ran low or the hunting was bad, or possibly out of a mingled boredom and hatred of the Mexicans for their depredations against the people. And the inevitable consequence of the raid was that there would be casualties, especially since the Mexican villagers were always better armed than the Chiricahuas. Chiricahua culture required a death to be avenged, and so a grieving Chiricahua brave was sooner or later obliged to recruit a party to take the warpath down into Mexico, to Janos or Casas Grandes or Nacozari or Carrizal. Exacting their revenge, the party would disappear northward again into mountainous retreats where only other Apaches would dare to go. And then the raid, the casualties, the warpath, and the old cycle kicked over again.

By the time the white Americans were declaring their independence from *their* imperialist oppressors, the Spanish had been at war with these red guerrillas for over a century —a century of raids, killings, punitive expeditions, isolated murders, despoiled pack trains, bodies rotting in the sun or frozen like cordwood in the high mountains. Now they began a determined drive destined to push the Apaches northward out of Mexico into areas where they were attacked by their hereditary enemies, the Comanches. Caught in such an accidental pincers movement, the Apaches dwindled in numbers but not in toughness.

From childhood they raised their males to be tireless, deep-chested runners, skilled rustlers, resourceful hiders, agile hand-to-hand combatants. Their women were expected to be adept at striking a camp quickly, establishing a new one, and equally skilled at raising children and tending to the horses. In the bitter years of the white-Apache wars, some women also achieved honor as warriors who rode with the men.

As soon as I was old enough to understand, recalled an Apache man, "I was told who were our enemies." So began his apprenticeship in raiding and warfare. A Chiricahua, he learned, might often be at a disadvantage—outnumbered, unhorsed, outgunned—but he should never be outfought or outmaneuvered. "My son," his tutor in warfare would instruct him,

> you know no one will help you in this world. You must do something. You run to that mountain and come back. That will make you strong. My son, you know no one is your friend, not even your sister, your father, or your mother. Your legs are your friends; your brain is your friend; your eyesight is your friend; your hair is your friend; your hands are your friends; you must do something with them.

> Someday you will be with people who are starving. You will have to get something for them. If you go somewhere, you must beat the enemy who are attacking you before they get over the hill. . . . Before they beat you, you must get in front of them . . . and bring them back dead. Then all the people will be proud of you. Then you will be the only man. Then all the people will talk about you. That is why I talk to you in this way.

The boy learned to rise before dawn and run up a nearby mountain. Another morning he would be ordered into an icy stream. He was required to run four miles holding a mouthful of water without spilling or swallowing any. He took part in wrestling tournaments with his peers to acquire toughness and agility in hand-to-hand combat. He took part also in slingshot battles where the penalty for lack of agility might well be a broken bone or a blinded eye. All of this was supervised by a man recognized for his superior talents as a warrior, and he was a stern, relentless instructor, for he knew well this was not play he sponsored but a matter of life and death. One Chiricahua boy left oral testimony to how much he and his peers came to hate Geronimo for the rigors he had put them through when he supervised their training.

When at last the training was complete and the warrior-tutor was satisfied he had imparted all the knowledge he could, then he would step back and in a sense regard his pupil almost as if he were a work of art: a young man honed to the fineness of a bone-pointed missile and hungering to be talked of for exploits in battle. The Chiricahuas were not big (Mangas Coloradas and Cochise were notable exceptions), but even the American troopers who became their mortal adversaries acknowledged that no tougher, smarter, or more perfectly formed warriors ever fought. If the tribal culture aimed to produce a narrow and singular talent, and one that must give us a long pause for thought, it superlatively succeeded.

IV

Originally the Apaches seemed friendly to the white Americans, but this was probably because neither represented a threat to the other. This was in 1807, when Zeb Pike was stumbling around lost in the desert and probably glad to see some other people out there. Relations were bound to worsen with increased contact, considering the principals involved. In 1837 two white traders killed an Apache chief, but widespread trouble was averted.

It could not be averted after October 1860, from which time we can date the Apache wars ending only when Geronimo and Naiche surrendered the remnants of their band in the late summer of 1886. In that October, a man named Ward beat his half-breed son so savagely that the boy ran away. When Ward sobered up, he told everybody that the Chiricahua chief Cochise had stolen the boy and some stock as well. A punitive expedition was mounted by the soldiers, but before they could chastise Cochise he came in with his head men to protest his innocence.

Once the whites had these Chiricahuas inside the parley tent, however, they could not resist the temptation to capture them. A ring of soldiers closed up around the tent while, inside, Cochise was informed that he and his men would be held prisoners until the missing boy and the stock were returned. When he heard this, he whipped out his knife, slashed a hole in the tent, and leapt through it. The soldiers waiting outside were so surprised to see this tall Indian in their midst that they parted ranks like the Red Sea, and Cochise escaped. Soon after, he captured three whites as hostages and set about the business of long-distance negotiations to secure the release of his own men.

But the whites weren't bargaining, and in a rage at their stubbornness, treachery, and ignorance, Cochise dragged one of the hostages to death behind his horse while a detachment of soldiers looked on. Later, still unable to get his men back, the chief had the other two hostages killed. In reprisal the whites hanged the Chiricahua head men in February 1861. The Cochise wars were on, and for ten years the chief made whites in Arizona and New Mexico wish they had questioned that Mr. Ward more closely. (The runaway boy, by the way, was Mickey Free, who later became a scout in the final Chiricahua campaigns.)

Whereas for the Plains tribes the coming of the Civil War had meant a temporary if incomplete relief from the relentless pressure of the troops, for the Chiricahuas things during the war years were even more hazardous. Both Confederate and Union forces were in their area. Both sides offered bounties for Apache scalps, but the contemplated Confederate strategy against the Indians was somewhat more savage than that of their adversaries. In instructions to the commander of the Arizona Guards in 1862, Confederate Governor John R. Baylor wrote:

I learn from Lieutenant J. J. Jackson that Indians have been in your post for the purpose of making a treaty. The Congress of the Confederate States has passed a law declaring extermination to all hostile Indians. You will therefore use all means to persuade the Apaches or any tribe to come in for the purpose of making peace, and when you get them together kill all the grown Indians and take the children prisoners and sell them to defray the expense of killing the Indians. Buy whisky and such other goods as may be necessary for the Indians and I will order vouchers given to cover the amount expended. Leave nothing undone to insure success, and have a sufficient number of men around to allow no Indian to escape.

Fortunately for the Apaches, higher Confederate command found this plan too brutal, and it was never put into practice, though it was suggested that at such future time as was practicable the Apaches be "legally enslaved."

In January 1863, Mangas Coloradas was treacherously taken prisoner and assassinated in what Geronimo calls the "greatest wrong ever done to the Indians." (Like many Indians, Geronimo assumed that "Indian" and his tribe's name were synonymous; in the case of many tribes there is but one word for both the tribal name and the word meaning human beings.) Though this blow for progress was struck by the Grand Army of the Republic, surely the Confederates would have approved its style, which is amply described in Geronimo's narrative. Other similar acts of dishonesty—such as treating Apaches to a gift of piñon nuts seasoned with strychnine

—continued during the war years, but at war's end the final solution to the Apache problem was not in sight.

It might have emerged in a less grim fashion than it finally did had the Chiricahuas and other Apache groups been given the generous reservations and hunting preserves that Thomas Jeffords and a few other farseeing whites had requested for them. It was Jeffords who at last won the respect of the great Cochise and cooled the fires of his hatred so much that the chief was finally willing to bring his bands in near a reservation at Fort Bowie. Other Apache groups had already agreed to settle on reservations, but what happened at Fort Grant, Arizona, in the same year that Cochise and his Chiricahuas laid down their arms cannot have inspired them with much confidence.

At the end of April 1871, a group of 146 assassins marched from Tucson and fell upon the sleeping camp of the Arivaipa Apaches at peace on the Camp Grant Reservation. Papago Indians, Mexicans, and leading white citizens from Tucson stole in among the wickiups and began the silent butchering with heavy clubs and knives. A few minutes later when the camp became aroused, rifles did the work, and within a half hour the job was finished: an estimated 108 Apaches killed, only eight of whom were men, the rest of the males being off hunting. Later a trial was arranged for those implicated in the "fight"; a jury deliberated twenty minutes before returning an acquittal.

Can we better understand, then, that deep distrust of all whites that so clearly characterizes Geronimo, Victorio (also spelled Victoria), Naiche (also spelled Natchez), Juh (also Who and Whoa), and the Chiricahuas during the 1870s and '80s? And of all the distrustful, the intransigent, the wild, the worst from the white point of view was Geronimo, because he was the best from the standpoint of Chiricahua culture. Among a people whose way of life was the raid and for whom the war of vengeance was the inevitable aftermath, Geronimo rose to prominence as a raider and warrior. Among a people who worshiped the land, Geronimo's attachment to his territory became legendary.

So successful in raiding and warring did he become that he can best be described within Chiricahua culture as a war shaman. In Chiricahua culture, shamanism abounded and the possession of a ceremony, big or small, made one a shaman, but in times of strife the man who knew ceremonies for effectively dealing with enemies would be particularly important. It is clear that, for the Chiricahuas, strife was a way of life, but with the white Americans pressing them throughout the '60s and '70s, tension and strife rose to new levels, and so did Geronimo. With the Chiricahuas' way of life threatened as it had never been before, this man came forward to a position of leadership at least equal to that of a hereditary chief, which he was not.

Geronimo's way was the *old* Chiricahua way, and nothing he saw in the behavior or actions of whites convinced him that Cochise was right in bringing his bands in to the reservation. Certainly he saw nothing very attractive in the style of life which the whites had marked out for the Chiricahuas once they got them on the reservation. They had never been very extensive or serious farmers, probably because they moved about so much; now they were to be exclusively tillers of the soil. The raid and the war of vengeance were now to be ended. A Chiricahua male could not beat his wife for misdeeds, nor could he cut off the end of her nose if he found her unfaithful. Nor could he even make *tizwin*, the maize-based beer of which he was so fond. In short, the Chiricahuas were to become pretend whites without being able really to share in the white man's culture. They were to be prisoners in all but name.

These things went hard with the Chiricahuas, and especially the men, but they went harder with Geronimo than with anyone else, again because he was himself the perfection of the Chiricahua way. Others, less perfect—or with clearer vision, as history tells us now—preferred to make these difficult accommodations, and there is enough evidence to indicate that Geronimo was both hated and feared by some of his people because of his uncompromising behavior. In his autobiography he tells us as much when he recounts his early days as a warrior leading expeditions down into Old Mexico, but in the '70s and '80s he used tricks, lies, and sometimes outright kidnapping to get his people to continue to fight against the whites—and this he did *not* choose to tell his white editor.

In April 1876, Geronimo led a band of Chiricahuas off the San Carlos reservation in the first of his major transgressions against the new white way. For almost exactly a year he remained what the whites would call "at large," which is to say that he lived the old Chiricahua way, but with a new focus of venom—the whites, who seemed more determined to rub his people out than the Mexicans ever had been. As the *Arizona Citizen* pungently put it in the immediate aftermath of the breakout, "the kind of war needed for the Chiricahua Apaches is steady[,] unrelenting[,] hopeless, and undiscriminating war, slaying men, women, and children . . . until every valley and crest and crag and fastness shall send to high heaven the grateful incense of festering and rotting Chiricahuas." This was hardly beating around the bush, but what the paper chose not to say was that frontier opinion had never believed in the reservation system, even for tribes far more

24

docile than Geronimo's Chiricahuas. In New Mexico and Arizona potentially rich deposits of ore had been discovered, prospectors and then mining companies were rushing into the region, and instant settlements were popping up all over what had very recently been Apache lands. Plainly, these lands were now needed by a civilized people, and even a reservation so comparatively modest in size as San Carlos was a flagrant waste of commercially valuable real estate.

Moreover, the paper's readers, the new residents of those instant settlements, were anything but Indian lovers. They were instead rough men and women, often violent, and many of them had failed in the settled lands back east. As Crevecoeur had observed more than a century earlier, it was not the prosperous and successful who emigrated from the settled lands to become frontiersmen. It was instead the poor and the desperate, and thus, he said, civilization's incursions into new territory were routinely made by the "most vicious of our people." A frontier ditty summed up the motley populace this way:

> Say, what was your name in the States?
> Was it Brown or Jackson or Bates?
> Did you murder your wife and fly for your life?
> Say, what was your name in the States?

No accurate assessment of the Chiricahuas' and Geronimo's problems with the whites can be made without due consideration of the prejudices of the Southwestern frontiersmen who so raucously called for Indian lives—and lands.

During his time off the reservation, Geronimo and his people did their full share of raiding and killing, though even this early it had become convenient for whites to hang almost every crime in the region around his neck. After some months when he was observed hanging around the Warm Springs agency with a new herd of a hundred horses, orders went out to John Clum, the agent at San Carlos, to go east into New Mexico and arrest him there. Clum was an arrogant and a vainglorious young man, but he was also energetic, intelligent, and resourceful, and when he went over to Warm Springs he made sure to bring along with him about a hundred well-armed Apache police, whom he secreted in the buildings surrounding the agency parade ground. When he was ready, he sent word to Geronimo's camp that he wanted to talk.

The war shaman and his people came into the agency on the morning of April 21, 1877, Geronimo grim-faced, his rifle across his arm, and confident he had the young White Eyes right where he wanted him. Speaking with only a small force showing, Clum told him he was here to arrest him and take him and his people back to San Carlos, where they belonged. As Geronimo listened to this through an interpreter, his scowl deepened and his thumb began to move toward the hammer of his rifle. "We are not going to San Carlos with you," Clum recalled him saying, "and unless you are very careful, you and your Apache police will not go back to San Carlos, either. Your bodies will stay here at Ojo Caliente to make food for coyotes." But Geronimo hadn't reckoned with Clum's hidden force, and now, at a prearranged signal, the rest of the Apache police burst from the agency buildings, rifles at the ready. Geronimo suddenly found himself surrounded, and in a few minutes Clum had him clapped in irons for the trip to San Carlos, where he languished in the stockade for several months. He was released at last only on the understanding that his roving days were over: this was where he would have to stay. Also, he would have to forsake the horse and the gun and go to work farming, an alien task, and one, it must be pointed out, that a good many whites in the region also found distasteful, preferring the possibility of striking it rich or at the very least the freedoms of cowpunching to picking at the dry soil with a hoe.

Geronimo learned to raise crops, and the agents claimed he became proud of the fruits of his husbandry. But in truth, few were fooled, and the white men who cared to look closely into the eyes of the captive shaman were not reassured by the unbanked fires they saw there: Geronimo was not a "good Indian" in any sense of the term, and certainly not in General Sheridan's. But since he was a prisoner his captors felt safe enough in taunting him, often drawing a line across their throats with their forefingers to signify what fate awaited him. Meanwhile, intertribal frictions mounted on the reservation as did intratribal ones between those who wanted to walk the white man's road (or felt there was no other choice) and those who stubbornly held out for the old ways, foreseeing no future for themselves as Indians under these conditions.

In September 1881, alarmed by recent developments on the reservation, including a sudden concentration of troops, Geronimo led another break from it, going south to the Sierra Madres, where so often in the old time the Apaches had been safe from all pursuit. But this was not the old time. Now there were enemies on all sides and many more of them, and now, too, the whites had put General George Crook into the field. Before, when the army had tried tracking the Apaches into the mountains, it had been like "chasing deer with a brass band," as one officer ruefully put it. But Crook quickly understood that only Apaches could successfully track Apaches, and when he began his pursuit of Geronimo he did so with a predominantly native force. Only Apaches, Crook found, had what it took to persevere in that often unforgiving landscape; and where the army would have had to give up, the Apache scouts knew how to keep on going. At the end of

May 1883, Crook and his force ran Geronimo's people to earth and got them to agree to return to San Carlos, though he did give them a two-month grace period to round up groups scattered through the crags.

It was almost a year later when Geronimo showed up at the border, and he announced his coming by a mile-high cloud of dust rising from under the hooves of cattle and horses he had stolen from the Mexicans during these months. If the whites placed such a premium on riches, he was at least going back to their world well supplied with these. Alas, they were all taken from him at San Carlos.

Now it was even tougher to live on the reservation than it had been before: it was overcrowded; there were even more serious intertribal antagonisms; and as for Geronimo, he was a man with a reputation. Still, as he played at farming, he schemed for a way to get his people together again for a large break that might destroy the reservation system forever. As usual in situations of this sort, the whites were playing right into the warrior's hands: they were ever ready to give the natives cause to revolt by being utterly ruthless in their attempts to destroy tribal culture. In this instance it was the issues of *tizwin* drinking and wife beating that brought about the confrontation Geronimo had been seeking.

In the middle of May 1885, with the situation at San Carlos tense over these issues, Geronimo told Naiche and another chief, Chihuahua, that Lieutenant Britton Davis and Chatto, a friendly Chiricahua chief, had been murdered and that the whites were going to arrest the three of them for the crime. In fact, the murders had never taken place, though Geronimo had instructed two warriors to commit them once the break had been made. Geronimo's plan worked, and the three men and a sizable band left the reservation and traveled toward Old Mexico. But as an indication of how the tide was running, when Naiche and Chihuahua discovered how they had been tricked into this act of defiance they came near to killing Geronimo.

Again General Crook was sent into the field, and again he found the Chiricahuas after an incredible campaign, which ended—or at the time *seemed* to have ended—with Crook's famous conference with Geronimo and the chiefs at El Cañon de los Embudos, March 25 and 27, 1886. The conference became famous not only because it was thought to have represented the final capitulation of the man who had come to be the Bad Injun in the white American mind, but also because it was attended by a photographer and a reporter. C. S. Fly, one of the West's most intrepid photographers, made the trip to the canyon and brought back a series of remarkable pictures, the best known of which shows the whites seated in an open-ended circle with their quarry, Geronimo, squatting in the center, looking small against these big bearded men. From the accidental composition of the photograph, however, you would think he was a meteorite just dropped into their midst. In the background lurk the armed figures of his Chiricahua warriors.

In terms of actual negotiations it was not much of a conference. The Chiricahuas were well supplied with guns, ammunition, and horses, all of which they had stolen since they jumped the reservation; but they were vastly outnumbered, they were hungry, and the people were getting tired of running. All except Geronimo. After Chihuahua and Naiche had come forward on the twenty-seventh to make rather abject surrender speeches to Crook, the old warrior himself, no chief and so not able to really speak for anyone but himself, came forward and in a few simple words gave up.

Two or three words are enough. I have little to say. I surrender to you. We are all comrades, all one family, all one band. What the others say I say also. I give myself up to you. Do with me what you please. I surrender. Once I moved around like the wind. Now I surrender to you and that is all.

That was all. The Chiricahua had been taken, and General Crook left for Fort Bowie with a satisfied heart. The Chiricahua retired to their camp a little way up in the hills, and the soldiers settled down to rest for the trip back to civilization.

None reckoned, however, with one of those inevitable harbingers of civilization, a man named Tribolet (or Tribollet), who had come out to the conference with a wagon full of whiskey and a tent to sell it in. The evidence of the next morning plainly showed that Geronimo and Naiche had bought heavily of the merchant's rotgut, doctored with tobacco and assorted trash to give it an authentic bite. Not only had Tribolet sold the Indians this stuff, but he had told them that once back on United States soil, they would be shot down by the troops. The combination of bad liquor, fears of ambush, and general distrust of whites proved far stronger than the handshakes with Crook of the day before, and when the caravan started off on March 28—the soldiers in the lead, the Chiricahuas following—Geronimo, Naiche, and a party of thirty-eight (some say thirty-nine) men, women, and children slipped away into the hills. The main party continued on, but Crook had lost his biggest catch.

One can perfectly imagine without the aid of official documents how Crook's immediate superior, Philip Sheridan, reacted to the loss of Geronimo. Crook resigned before he could be censured, and General Nelson A. Miles replaced him with orders to run the little band, already doing its full share of killing and looting, into the ground. A huge pursuit force was sent out with orders to kill or capture, preferably the former. This time there was to be no treating with the hostiles.

Miles gave effective command of this latest expedition to Captain H. W. Lawton of the Fourth Cavalry, who in turn wisely employed several old friends of Geronimo's. At that it took almost five months before Geronimo came in near Fronteras in Sonora to ask for peace. If there were terms offered, they were at best ambiguous, and Geronimo was hardly in a position to bargain for more binding promises: the people had simply had it. They were tired, ragged, starving, and finally their will to resist had been broken, the inevitable end of any clash between a people with a huge numerical and technological superiority and a tiny tribe essentially pretechnological.

When Geronimo and Naiche surrendered for the last time on September 4, 1886, and a few days later were put aboard a train for Florida, they were headed for a life of that pauperdom General Sherman had envisioned, even if they did not know it. The other once-hostile Chiricahuas had already been put aboard another train for Florida, leaving behind them at the railroad station their personal belongings, their horses, and their dogs, some of these latter forlornly running after the departing train and going on for twenty miles down the tracks. The train, that symbol of progress that had cut its way westward, split the bison herd in two, and joined the coasts of a continent, was now bearing into alien grounds the last remnants of the human barriers who had once for a brief moment thought to oppose something they never really understood.

The Chiricahuas never got back home, despite promises that had been made them and despite years of pleas that became ever more pathetic as time and exile lengthened. (Probably the main reason Geronimo finally agreed to tell his story to Barrett was the opportunity it gave him to address the white man's Great Father one more time on this subject.) After being imprisoned in Florida and Alabama, where more than a quarter of them died of tuberculosis, malaria, and simple despair, the remnant Apaches were granted a return to the West. Not to their homelands, though, as they had so long hoped, but to a military reservation, Fort Sill, Oklahoma. In the fall of 1894 they arrived there to begin all over again from scratch. Like so many of his people, Geronimo left behind the graves of family members, in his case a wife and two children.

Fort Sill was better than Fort Marion or Fort Pickens in Florida, and better too than Mount Vernon in Alabama that had seemed so oppressive to the prisoners with its thick forests and high humidity. Here at least they could see the sky and feel it, though initially the post commander had planned to pen them inside a high stockade until he was overruled by more humane superiors. Geronimo, however, remained a marked man, just as he had been since the mid-1870s, and none of his keepers at Fort Sill had anything good to say about him, even though he'd caused no trouble for a long time and had become one of the best of the Apache farmers. It was as if even so reduced—wearing his lumpy white man's costume, toiling in his little melon patch—he was still a threat, his face and eyes yet untamed and offering a continual challenge. The soldiers on the post called him "Gerry," because they knew he detested the name. But they all knew who he was and what.

Off the post the old man had become something of a celebrity, and he was quick to exploit his new status. Eastward in the country, where Indians were but a fast-fading memory, Geronimo could be regarded with a nostalgic thrill: a photogenic reminder of the wild days gone by and a trophy of white civilization's triumph over a wilderness continent. In 1898 he was put on exhibit at the Trans-Mississippi and International Exposition at Omaha, and on the train trip there he cut the buttons from his coat and sold them at stops along the way. When the train moved on to its next stop he sewed on new buttons from a supply he had brought with him. In the summer of 1901 he was taken to the Pan-American Exposition in Buffalo, and he was still there when President McKinley was fatally wounded. What he thought about this violence to the Great Father was not recorded, but he kept right on hawking the bows and arrows he had made, until he was taken back to Fort Sill. By the time he was taken to the St. Louis World's Fair in 1904, he had learned to print his name and would do so for money. The next year he rode in Teddy Roosevelt's inaugural parade alongside Quanah Parker, another redskin whose name once had struck fear into frontier hearts, and American Horse, the Ogalala Lakota who'd survived the Ghost Dance hysteria and the ensuing massacre at Wounded Knee. When they clip-clopped down Pennsylvania Avenue past the reviewing stand, people in the dense crowd hollered, "Hooray for Geronimo!" and tossed their hats in the air.

V

Over the years since Geronimo died at Fort Sill in 1909, his name and that of the Apaches have lived on in an odd variety of ways. So too have the attitudes that pushed the Chiricahuas and most other tribes to the very brink of cultural extinction. World War II paratroopers hollered the old warrior's name as they leapt from their planes over enemy territory, while kids leaping from the high board at public pools did the same.

And, of course, Geronimo has been invoked in an apparently endless string of Hollywood oaters that, even when sympathetic (as nowadays they tend to be), trade on a name that still is equated with "savage." The same holds true for the tribal name "Apache," which has even crossed the Atlantic to enter the French language, where it denotes a Parisian thug.

As for the attitudes, they are to be most forcefully encountered west of the Mississippi, which was to have been Indian country forever. Out where most of the large reservations are located and where most of the public lands are too, there is still a steady, settled hatred of Native Americans that gathers in intensity the nearer you get to a reservation, and there is still a white desire to take what little land they have left. "My solution to the Indian problem?" a school official rhetorically asked on the Navajo reservation. "Turn 'em out. Make 'em Americans." Spend a day and a night in the town nearest any reservation, and you will hear—and see—anti-Indian prejudice that has not lost that much of its vigor since Geronimo and his people were deported to the East.

The same sentiment that favors the termination of the tribes' reservation status also applies to our public lands, our national parks, and our national forests, though here it is hard to see how even in private hands the lumber companies could get more out of them. Ever since the public domain came into existence, it has been the object of a steady, relentless attack by private interests in a campaign that tellingly resembles the one called for by that Arizona newspaper against the Chiricahuas back in 1876. In the West the federal government and its minions, the BLM, the Park Service, the Forest Service, and the Department of the Interior, are regularly stigmatized as the mindless enemies of free enterprise, and in an odd, ironic way they almost seem to have taken the place of the savages, threatening the livelihood of the hard-pressed settlers.

It is tempting to suggest that Geronimo and Sitting Bull and Red Cloud would understand this, would see it as another aspect of that same mind-set they faced back in the nineteenth century. And in fact, many of those in the West calling for the breakup of the reservations and the dispersal of the public lands, national parks, and forests proudly identify themselves as descendants of those who won the West. And now that almost all of the West is theirs, it proves not to be enough: there is always some more that might be had. Red Cloud might have come closest to articulating the situation when, after he knew further resistance was futile, he allegedly told a white delegation, "We didn't need all this land, and neither did you."

Frederick Turner
Santa Fe, New Mexico

A Note on the Text

GERONIMO told the story of his life in 1905–6 to Asa (Ace) Daklugie, the son of Juh (Who, Whoa), a hostile chief who fought with Geronimo in the last campaigns and who drowned in a stream outside of Casas Grandes, Sonora, in 1886; he had gotten drunk on mescal during a peace mission. Daklugie, who had received some education at the Carlisle Indian School, translated the story for S. M. Barrett, a white who was then superintendent of education in nearby Lawton, Oklahoma.

During the storytelling sessions, Geronimo would range freely over the events of his life in a manner characteristic of many American aboriginal narratives. This manner consists of telling only that which seems to the teller important and telling it in the fashion and the order which seems to him appropriate. I emphasize this because it is clear that certain rearrangements of the materials would make a more coherent narrative. Yet this would not be the aboriginal style of extended narratives, and so it would be false to make such changes. I have resisted the temptation, and Geronimo's narrative stands as Barrett published it. I have, however, deleted some of Barrett's obviously superfluous material: in his Introduction, the narration of his dealings with the War Depart-

37

ment; and in the body, his account of Apache-white warfare in the nineteenth century.

As to the accuracy of the whole, let us say to begin with that Geronimo, for reasons of his own, did not choose to tell Barrett everything. He was, after all, still a prisoner of war, and he was a bitter man who regretted to the end of his life that he had surrendered to Miles rather than fighting it out in the mountains. Considering his treatment in subsequent years, one cannot much blame him. At any rate, there are numerous gaps and omissions in his narrative, and wherever possible I have tried to supply the relevant factual data in footnotes followed by my initials (FT). In some cases, particularly those events before Geronimo came to the attention of whites, it is simply impossible to comment on what he says. I have left the majority of Barrett's footnotes (followed by his initials) as they originally occurred, even though these are occasionally inaccurate.

Geronimo died February 17, 1909, in the military hospital at Fort Sill. Frank Lockwood reports that he interviewed an official of the Dutch Reformed Church who said that a few days before his death Geronimo had gone to nearby Lawton to sell one of the bows he was always making. There he got drunk with the money from the sale and, while returning "home," fell out of his buggy and lay all night on the road in a freezing rain. He was discovered the next day and taken to the hospital, where he died. By his own reckoning, Geronimo was about eighty. If one accepts Debo's earlier birthdate of 1823, he would have been eighty-six. As a young man he had a vision in which a spirit voice told him bullets could never kill him, and so it proved, though his body was riddled with more than half a dozen wounds. He died a prisoner of war.

Introductory

I first met Geronimo in the summer of 1904, when I acted for him as interpreter of English into Spanish, and vice versa, in selling a war bonnet. After that he always had a pleasant word for me when we met, but never entered into a general conversation with me until he learned that I had once been wounded by a Mexican. As soon as he was told of this, he came to see me and expressed freely his opinion of the average Mexican and his aversion to all Mexicans in general.

I invited him to visit me again, which he did, and upon his invitation, I visited him at his tepee in the Fort Sill Military reservation.

In the summer of 1905, Dr. J. M. Greenwood, superintendent of schools at Kansas City, Missouri, visited me, and I took him to see the chief. Geronimo was quite formal and reserved until Dr. Greenwood said, "I am a friend of General Howard, whom I have heard speak of you." "Come," said Geronimo, and led the way to a shade, had seats brought for us, put on his war bonnet, and served watermelon *à l'Apache* (cut in big chunks), while he talked freely and cheerfully. When we left he gave us a pressing invitation to visit him again.

In a few days the old chief came to see me and asked

about "my father." I said, "You mean the old gentleman from Kansas City—he has returned to his home." "He is your father?" said Geronimo. "No," I said, "my father died twenty-five years ago. Dr. Greenwood is only my friend." After a moment's silence the old Indian spoke again, this time in a tone of voice intended to carry conviction, or at least to allow no further discussion. "Your natural father is dead, this man has been your friend and adviser from youth. By adoption *he is your father*. Tell him he is welcome to come to my home at any time." It was of no use to explain any more, for the old man had determined not to understand my relation to Dr. Greenwood except in accordance with Indian customs, and I let the matter drop.

In the latter part of that summer I asked the old chief to allow me to publish some of the things he had told me, but he objected, saying, however, that if I would pay him, and if the officers in charge did not object, he would tell me the whole story of his life.[1] I immediately called at the fort (Fort Sill) and asked the officer in charge, Lieutenant Purington, for permission to write the life of Geronimo. I was promptly informed that the privilege would not be granted. Lieutenant Purington explained to me the many depredations committed by Geronimo and his warriors, and the enormous cost of subduing the Apaches, adding that the old Apache deserved to be hanged rather than spoiled by so much attention from civilians. A suggestion from me that our government had paid many soldiers and officers to go to Arizona and kill Geronimo and the Apaches, and that they did not seem to know how to do it, did not prove very gratifying to the pride of the regular army officer, and I decided to seek elsewhere for per-

[1] Typical of Geronimo's behavior in the late years of his captivity. He had learned the hard way how much money counted in the white man's culture and would do little for the whites without pay. (FT)

mission. Accordingly I wrote to President Roosevelt that here was an old Indian who had been held a prisoner of war for twenty years and had never been given a chance to tell his side of the story, and asked that Geronimo be granted permission to tell for publication, in his own way, the story of his life, and that he be guaranteed that the publication of his story would not affect unfavorably the Apache prisoners of war. By return mail I received word that the authority had been granted. In a few days I received word from Fort Sill that the President had ordered the officer in charge to grant permission as requested. An interview was requested that I might receive the instructions of the War Department. When I went to Fort Sill the officer in command handed me a brief, which constituted my instructions.

Early in October I secured the services of an educated Indian, Asa Daklugie, son of Whoa, chief of the Nedni Apaches, as interpreter, and the work of compiling the book began.

Geronimo refused to talk when a stenographer was present, or to wait for corrections or questions when telling the story. Each day he had in mind what he would tell and told it in a very clear, brief manner. He might prefer to talk at his own tepee, at Asa Daklugie's house, in some mountain dell, or as he rode in a swinging gallop across the prairie; whenever his fancy led him, there he told whatever he wished to tell and no more.[2] On the day that he first gave any portion of his autobiography he would not be questioned about any details, nor would he add another word, but simply said, "Write what I have spoken," and left us to remember and write the story without one bit of assistance. He would agree, however,

[2] This is the style of so many extended Indian narratives that I venture to call it characteristic. It has long been clear that there are important differences between the styles of oral and written narratives. (FT)

to come on another day to my study, or any place designated by me, and listen to the reproduction (in Apache) of what had been told, and at such times would answer all questions or add information wherever he could be convinced that it was necessary.

He soon became so tired of book making that he would have abandoned the task but for the fact that he had agreed to tell the complete story. When he once gives his word, nothing will turn him from fulfilling his promise. A very striking illustration of this was furnished by him early in January, 1906. He had agreed to come to my study on a certain date, but at the appointed hour the interpreter came alone, and said that Geronimo was very sick with cold and fever. He had come to tell me that we must appoint another date, as he feared the old warrior had an attack of pneumonia. It was a cold day and the interpreter drew a chair up to the grate to warm himself after the exposure of the long ride. Just as he was seating himself he looked out of the window, then rose quickly, and without speaking pointed to a rapidly moving object coming our way. In a moment I recognized the old chief riding furiously (evidently trying to arrive as soon as the interpreter did), his horse flecked with foam and reeling from exhaustion. Dismounting he came in and said in a hoarse whisper, "I promised to come. I am here."

I explained to him that I had not expected him to come on such a stormy day, and that in his physical condition he must not try to work. He stood for some time, and then without speaking left the room, remounted his tired pony, and with bowed head faced ten long miles of cold north wind—he had kept his promise.

When he had finished his story I submitted the manuscript to Major Charles W. Taylor, Eighteenth Cavalry, commandant, Fort Sill, Oklahoma, who gave me some valuable sug-

"How the Book Was Made." From the left, S. M. Barrett, Geronimo, and interpreter Asa Daklugie, second cousin of Geronimo. *(PHOTOGRAPH FROM THE ORIGINAL EDITION. COURTESY OF THE CENTER FOR SOUTHWEST RESEARCH, GENERAL LIBRARY, UNIVERSITY OF NEW MEXICO)*

gestions as to additional related information which I asked Geronimo to give. In most cases the old chief gave the desired information, but in some instances he refused, stating his reasons for so doing.

When the added information had been incorporated I submitted the manuscript to President Roosevelt, from whose letter I quote: "This is a very interesting volume which you have in manuscript, but I would advise that you disclaim responsibility in all cases where the reputation of an individual is assailed."

In accordance with that suggestion, I have appended notes throughout the book disclaiming responsibility for adverse criticisms of any persons mentioned by Geronimo.

On June 2d, 1906, I transmitted the complete manuscript to the War Department. The following quotation is from the letter of transmission:

"In accordance with endorsement number eight of the 'Brief' submitted to me by the commanding officer of Fort Sill, which endorsement constituted the instructions of the Department, I submit herewith manuscript of the Autobiography of Geronimo.

"The manuscript has been submitted to the President, and at his suggestion I have disclaimed any responsibility for the criticisms (made by Geronimo) of individuals mentioned."

Six weeks after the manuscript was forwarded, Thomas C. Barry, Brigadier General, Assistant to the Chief of Staff, sent to the President the following:

"MEMORANDUM FOR THE SECRETARY OF WAR.
"Subject: Manuscript of the Autobiography of Geronimo. The paper herewith, which was referred to this office on July

6th, with instructions to report as to whether there is anything objectionable in it, is returned.

"The manuscript is an interesting autobiography of a notable Indian, made by himself. There are a number of passages which, from the departmental point of view, are decidedly objectionable. These are found on pages 73, 74, 90, 91, and 97, and are indicated by marginal lines in red. The entire manuscript appears in a way important as showing the Indian side of a prolonged controversy, but it is believed that the document, either in whole or in part, should not receive the approval of the War Department."

The memorandum is published that the objections of the War Department may be made known to the public.

The objection is raised to the mention on page 122 of the book of an attack upon Indians in a tent at Apache Pass or Bowie, by U.S. soldiers. The statement of Geronimo is, however, substantially confirmed by L. C. Hughes, editor of *The Star*, Tucson, Arizona.

On pages 135–6 and 139 of the book, Geronimo criticized General Crook. This criticism is simply Geronimo's private opinion of General Crook. We deem it a personal matter and leave it without comment, as it in no way concerns the history of the Apaches.

On page 143 of the book Geronimo accuses General Miles of bad faith. Of course, General Miles made the treaty with the Apaches, but we know very well that he is not responsible for the way the Government subsequently treated the prisoners of war. However, Geronimo cannot understand this and fixes upon General Miles the blame for what he calls unjust treatment.

One could not expect the Department of War to approve adverse criticisms of its own acts, but it is especially gratifying that such a liberal view has been taken of these criticisms, and also that such a frank statement of the merits of the Autobiography is submitted in the memorandum. Of course neither the President nor the War Department is in any way responsible for what Geronimo says; he has simply been granted the opportunity to state his own case as he sees it.

The fact that Geronimo has told the story in his own way is doubtless the only excuse necessary to offer for the many unconventional features of this work.

PART I

THE APACHES

1

Origin of the Apache Indians

In the beginning the world was covered with darkness. There was no sun, no day. The perpetual night had no moon or stars.

There were, however, all manner of beasts and birds. Among the beasts were many hideous, nameless monsters, as well as dragons, lions, tigers, wolves, foxes, beavers, rabbits, squirrels, rats, mice, and all manner of creeping things such as lizards and serpents. Mankind could not prosper under such conditions, for the beasts and serpents destroyed all human offspring.

All creatures had the power of speech and were gifted with reason.

There were two tribes of creatures: the birds or the feathered tribe and the beasts. The former were organized under their chief, the eagle.

These tribes often held councils, and the birds wanted light admitted. This the beasts repeatedly refused to do. Finally the birds made war against the beasts.

The beasts were armed with clubs, but the eagle had taught his tribe to use bows and arrows. The serpents were so wise that they could not all be killed. One took refuge in a perpendicular cliff of a mountain in Arizona, and his eye (changed into a brilliant stone) may be seen in that rock to this day. The bears, when killed, would each be changed into several other bears, so that the more bears the feathered tribe killed, the more there were. The dragon could not be killed, either, for he was covered with four coats of horny scales, and the arrows would not penetrate these. One of the most hideous, vile monsters (nameless) was proof against arrows, so the eagle flew high up in the air with a round, white stone, and let it fall on this monster's head, killing him instantly. This was such a good service that the stone was called sacred.[1] They fought for many days, but at last the birds won the victory.

After this war was over, although some evil beasts remained, the birds were able to control the councils, and light was admitted. Then mankind could live and prosper. The eagle was chief in this good fight: therefore, his feathers were worn by man as emblems of wisdom, justice, and power.

Among the few human beings that were yet alive was a woman who had been blessed with many children, but these had always been destroyed by the beasts. If by any means she succeeded in eluding the others, the dragon, who was very wise and very evil, would come himself and eat her babes.

After many years a son of the rainstorm was born to her and she dug for him a deep cave.[2] The entrance to this cave

---

[1] A symbol of this stone is used in the tribal game of Kah. See Chapter IV. (SMB)

[2] In the Chiricahua creation myth which Geronimo tells here the woman's name is White Painted Woman. The heroic child is called Child of the Water since his father was Water in the form of a rainstorm. The other principal character is Killer of Enemies, usually referred to as the child's brother rather than his uncle as here. Interestingly, Geronimo portrays Killer of Enemies as

she closed and over the spot built a camp fire. This concealed the babe's hiding place and kept him warm. Every day she would remove the fire and descend into the cave, where the child's bed was, to nurse him; then she would return and rebuild the camp fire.

Frequently the dragon would come and question her, but she would say, "I have no more children; you have eaten all of them."

When the child was larger he would not always stay in the cave, for he sometimes wanted to run and play. Once the dragon saw his tracks. Now this perplexed and enraged the old dragon, for he could not find the hiding place of the boy; but he said that he would destroy the mother if she did not reveal the child's hiding place. The poor mother was very much troubled; she could not give up her child, but she knew the power and cunning of the dragon, therefore she lived in constant fear.

Soon after this the boy said that he wished to go hunting. The mother would not give her consent. She told him of the dragon, the wolves, and the serpents; but he said, "To-morrow I go."

At the boy's request his uncle (who was the only man then living) made a little bow and some arrows for him, and the two went hunting the next day. They trailed the deer far up the mountain and finally the boy killed a buck. His uncle showed him how to dress the deer and broil the meat. They broiled two hind quarters, one for the child and one for his uncle. When the meat was done they placed it on some bushes to cool. Just then the huge form of the dragon ap-

---

cowardly, for in another episode of this myth this character chooses the things which the whites will use in life while Child of the Water chooses those things for the Chiricahua. (FT)

peared. The child was not afraid, but his uncle was so dumb
with fright that he did not speak or move.

The dragon took the boy's parcel of meat and went aside
with it. He placed the meat on another bush and seated himself beside it. Then he said, "This is the child I have been
seeking. Boy, you are nice and fat, so when I have eaten this
venison I shall eat you." The boy said, "No, you shall not
eat me, and you shall not eat that meat." So he walked over
to where the dragon sat and took the meat back to his own
seat. The dragon said, "I like your courage, but you are fool-
ish; what do you think you could do?" "Well," said the boy,
"I can do enough to protect myself, as you may find out."
Then the dragon took the meat again, and then the boy re-
took it. Four times in all the dragon took the meat, and after
the fourth time the boy replaced the meat he said, "Dragon,
will you fight me?" The dragon said, "Yes, in whatever way
you like." The boy said, "I will stand one hundred paces
distant from you and you may have four shots at me with
your bow and arrows, provided that you will then exchange
places with me and give me four shots." "Good," said the
dragon. "Stand up."

Then the dragon took his bow, which was made of a large
pine tree. He took four arrows from his quiver; they were
made of young pine tree saplings, and each arrow was twenty
feet in length. He took deliberate aim, but just as the arrow
left the bow the boy made a peculiar sound and leaped into
the air. Immediately the arrow was shivered into a thousand
splinters, and the boy was seen standing on the top of a bright
rainbow over the spot where the dragon's aim had been directed. Soon the rainbow was gone and the boy was standing
on the ground again. Four times this was repeated, then the
boy said, "Dragon, stand here: it is my time to shoot." The
dragon said, "All right; your little arrows cannot pierce my

first coat of horn, and I have three other coats—shoot away." The boy shot an arrow, striking the dragon just over the heart, and one coat of the great horny scales fell to the ground. The next shot another coat, and then another, and the dragon's heart was exposed. Then the dragon trembled, but could not move. Before the fourth arrow was shot the boy said, "Uncle, you are dumb with fear; you have not moved; come here or the dragon will fall on you." His uncle ran toward him. Then he sped the fourth arrow with true aim, and it pierced the dragon's heart. With a tremendous roar the dragon rolled down the mountain side—down four precipices into a cañon below.

Immediately storm clouds swept the mountains, lightning flashed, thunder rolled, and the rain poured. When the rainstorm had passed, far down in the cañon below, they could see fragments of the huge body of the dragon lying among the rocks, and the bones of this dragon may still be found there.

This boy's name was Apache. Usen[3] taught him how to prepare herbs for medicine, how to hunt, and how to fight. He was the first chief of the Indians and wore the eagle's feathers as the sign of justice, wisdom, and power. To him, and to his people, as they were created, Usen gave homes in the land of the West.

[3] "Usen" is the Apache word for God. It is used here because it implies the attributes of deity that are held in their primitive religion. "Apache" means "Enemy." (SMB)

2

SUBDIVISIONS OF THE APACHE TRIBE

The Apache Indians are divided into six subtribes. To one of these, the Be-don-ko-he, I belong.[1]

Our tribe inhabited that region of mountainous country which lies west from the east line of Arizona, and south from the headwaters of the Gila River.

East of us lived the Chi-hen-ne (Ojo Caliente), (Hot Springs) Apaches. Our tribe never had any difficulty with them. Victoria, their chief, was always a friend to me. He always helped our tribe when we asked him for help. He lost

[1] Throughout this complicated discussion Geronimo is largely talking about the various bands and local groups of the Chiricahua Apaches; one such band was sometimes (and confusingly) called the Chiricahuas. A band, according to Opler (*An Apache Life-Way*) "is a division of the tribe based on territory, including within its borders those local groups near enough to unite for military action if the need arises or to cooperate for any important social occasion." The Bedonkohe whom Geronimo calls his own people appear to have been such a band. (FT)

CHIRICAHUA

Taza, eldest son of Cochise and his successor. He died in Washington, D.C., in 1876 while with a delegation to speak with President Ulysses Grant. Some Chiricahuas always believed the whites had murdered him. From a photograph by Ben Wittick. *(COURTESY OF THE SMITHSONIAN INSTITUTION: NATIONAL ANTHROPOLOGICAL ARCHIVES)*

his life in the defense of the rights of his people.[2] He was a good man and a brave warrior. His son Charlie now lives here in this reservation with us.

North of us lived the White Mountain Apaches. They were not always on the best of terms with our tribe, yet we seldom had any war with them. I knew their chief, Hash-ka-ai-la, personally, and I considered him a good warrior. Their range was next to that of the Navajo Indians, who were not of the same blood as the Apaches. We held councils with all Apache tribes, but never with the Navajo Indians. However, we traded with them and sometimes visited them.

To the west of our country ranged the Chi-e-a-hen Apaches. They had two chiefs within my time, Co-si-to and Co-da-hoo-yah. They were friendly, but not intimate with our tribe.

South of us lived the Cho-kon-en (Chiricahua) Apaches, whose chief in the old days was Co-chise, and later his son, Naiche. This tribe was always on the most friendly terms with us. We were often in camp and on the trail together. Naiche, who was my companion in arms, is now my companion in bondage.

To the south and west of us lived the Ned-ni Apaches. Their chief was Whoa, called by the Mexicans Capitan Whoa. They were our firm friends. The land of this tribe lies partly in Old Mexico and partly in Arizona.[3] Whoa and I often

---

[2] Killed by Mexican troops, October 14, 1880, after several months of running warfare. Faulk (*The Geronimo Campaign*) writes that one Mauricio Corredor killed Victoria (also, and more regularly, Victorio); this same individual is said to have killed Captain Emmet Crawford, January 11, 1886, while the latter was pursuing Geronimo in the Sierra Madre. (FT)

[3] The boundary lines established at different times between Mexico and the United States did not conform to the boundary lines of these Apache tribes, of course, and the Indians soon saw and took advantage of the international questions arising from the conflicting interests of the two governments. (SMB)

camped and fought side by side as brothers. My enemies were his enemies, my friends his friends. He is dead now, but his son Asa is interpreting this story for me.[4]

Still the four tribes (Bedonkohe, Chokonen, Chihenne, and Nedni), who were fast friends in the days of freedom, cling together as they decrease in number. Only the destruction of all our people would dissolve our bonds of friendship.

We are vanishing from the earth, yet I cannot think we are useless or Usen would not have created us. He created all tribes of men and certainly had a righteous purpose in creating each.

For each tribe of men Usen created He also made a home. In the land created for any particular tribe He placed whatever would be best for the welfare of that tribe.

When Usen created the Apaches He also created their homes in the West. He gave to them such grain, fruits, and game as they needed to eat. To restore their health when disease attacked them He made many different herbs to grow. He taught them where to find these herbs, and how to prepare them for medicine. He gave them a pleasant climate and all they needed for clothing and shelter was at hand.

Thus it was in the beginning: the Apaches and their homes each created for the other by Usen himself. When they are taken from these homes they sicken and die. How long[5] will it be until it is said, there are no Apaches?

---

[4] Whoa, also called Juh and Who, died in late May or early June, 1883, when returning from a peace mission at Casa Grandes. Some reports say that he was drunk when he fell from his mule into a stream and drowned, but his son Asa, who was with him at the time, says that he died of a heart attack. (FT)

[5] The Apache Indians held prisoners of war are greatly decreasing in numbers. There seems to be no particular cause, but nevertheless their numbers grow smaller. (SMB)

3

EARLY LIFE

I was born in No-doyohn Cañon, Arizona, June, 1829.

In that country which lies around the headwaters of the Gila River I was reared. This range was our fatherland; among these mountains our wigwams were hidden; the scattered valleys contained our fields; the boundless prairies, stretching away on every side, were our pastures; the rocky caverns were our burying places.

I was fourth in a family of eight children—four boys and four girls.[1] Of that family, only myself, my brother, Porico

---

[1] Geronimo is the fourth of a family of four boys and four girls. He has had four wives that were full-blooded Bedonkohe Apaches, and four that were part Bedonkohe Apache and part other Apache blood. Four of his children have been killed by Mexicans and four have been held in bondage by the U.S. Government. He firmly believes in destiny and in the magic of the number four. Besides Geronimo, only four full-blood Bedonkohe Apaches are now living. They are Porico (White Horse), Nah-de-ste, Mah-ta-neal, and To-klon-nen. (SMB)

White ortheography of Apache names is still primitive and must be regarded as only approximate. Angie Debo in *Geronimo: The Man, His Time, His Place* gives Nah-das-te for Geronimo's sister, here rendered as Nah-da-ste and Nah-de-ste. (FT)

(White Horse), and my sister, Nah-da-ste, are yet alive. We are held as prisoners of war in this Military Reservation (Fort Sill).

As a babe I rolled on the dirt floor of my father's tepee, hung in my tsoch (Apache name for cradle) at my mother's back, or suspended from the bough of a tree. I was warmed by the sun, rocked by the winds, and sheltered by the trees as other Indian babes.

When a child my mother taught me the legends of our people; taught me of the sun and sky, the moon and stars, the clouds and storms. She also taught me to kneel and pray to Usen for strength, health, wisdom, and protection. We never prayed against any person, but if we had aught against any individual we ourselves took vengeance. We were taught that Usen does not care for the petty quarrels of men.

My father had often told me of the brave deeds of our warriors, of the pleasures of the chase, and the glories of the warpath.

With my brothers and sisters I played about my father's home. Sometimes we played at hide-and-seek among the rocks and pines; sometimes we loitered in the shade of the cottonwood trees or sought the shudock (a kind of wild cherry) while our parents worked in the field. Sometimes we played that we were warriors. We would practice stealing upon some object that represented an enemy, and in our childish imitation often perform the feats of war. Sometimes we would hide away from our mother to see if she could find us, and often when thus concealed go to sleep and perhaps remain hidden for many hours.

When we were old enough to be of real service we went to the field with our parents: not to play, but to toil. When the crops were to be planted we broke the ground with wooden hoes. We planted the corn in straight rows, the beans among the corn, and the melons and pumpkins in irregular order over the field. We cultivated these crops as there was need.[2]

Our field usually contained about two acres of ground. The fields were never fenced. It was common for many families to cultivate land in the same valley and share the burden of protecting the growing crops from destruction by the ponies of the tribe, or by deer and other wild animals.

Melons were gathered as they were consumed. In the autumn pumpkins and beans were gathered and placed in bags or baskets; ears of corn were tied together by the husks, and then the harvest was carried on the backs of ponies up to our homes. Here the corn was shelled, and all the harvest stored away in caves or other secluded places to be used in winter.

We never fed corn to our ponies, but if we kept them up in the winter time we gave them fodder to eat. We had no cattle or other domestic animals except our dogs and ponies.

We did not cultivate tobacco, but found it growing wild. This we cut and cured in autumn, but if the supply ran out the leaves from the stalks left standing served our purpose. All Indians smoked—men and women.[3] No boy was allowed to smoke until he had hunted alone and killed large game— wolves and bears. Unmarried women were not prohibited from smoking, but were considered immodest if they did so. Nearly all matrons smoked.

Besides grinding the corn (by hand with stone mortars and pestles) for bread, we sometimes crushed it and soaked it,

[2] There is considerable dispute as to the practice of agriculture among the Chiricahua in pre-white times. They were nomadic but did settle for periods of time in a particular locale. And they could easily have learned planting and harvesting from the Mexicans. (FT)

[3] The Apaches did not smoke the peace pipe, unless it was proposed by some other Indians. They had no large pipes; in fact, they usually smoked cigarettes made by rolling the tobacco in wrappers of oak leaves. (SMB)

and after it had fermented made from this juice a "tis-win," which had the power of intoxication, and was very highly prized by the Indians. This work was done by the squaws and children. When berries or nuts were to be gathered the small children and the squaws would go in parties to hunt them, and sometimes stay all day. When they went any great distance from camp they took ponies to carry the baskets.

I frequently went with these parties, and upon one of these excursions a woman named Cho-ko-le got lost from the party and was riding her pony through a thicket in search of her friends. Her little dog was following as she slowly made her way through the thick underbrush and pine trees. All at once a grizzly bear rose in her path and attacked the pony. She jumped off and her pony escaped, but the bear attacked her, so she fought him the best she could with her knife. Her little dog, by snapping at the bear's heels and distracting his attention from the woman, enabled her for some time to keep pretty well out of his reach. Finally the grizzly struck her over the head, tearing off almost her whole scalp. She fell, but did not lose consciousness, and while prostrate struck him four good licks with her knife, and he retreated. After he had gone she replaced her torn scalp and bound it up as best she could, then she turned deathly sick and had to lie down. That night her pony came into camp with his load of nuts and berries, but no rider. The Indians hunted for her, but did not find her until the second day. They carried her home, and under the treatment of their medicine men all her wounds were healed.

The Indians knew what herbs to use for medicine, how to prepare them, and how to give the medicine. This they had been taught by Usen in the beginning, and each succeeding generation had men who were skilled in the art of healing.

In gathering the herbs, in preparing them, and in administering the medicine, as much faith was held in prayer as in the actual effect of the medicine. Usually about eight persons worked together in making medicine, and there were forms of prayer and incantations to attend each stage of the process. Four attended to the incantations and four to the preparation of the herbs.

Some of the Indians were skilled in cutting out bullets, arrow heads, and other missiles with which warriors were wounded. I myself have done much of this, using a common dirk or butcher knife.[4]

Small children wore very little clothing in winter and none in the summer. Women usually wore a primitive skirt, which consisted of a piece of cotton cloth fastened about the waist, and extending to the knees. Men wore breech cloths and moccasins. In winter they had shirts and leggings in addition.

Frequently when the tribe was in camp a number of boys and girls, by agreement, would steal away and meet at a place several miles distant, where they could play all day free from tasks. They were never punished for these frolics; but if their hiding places were discovered they were ridiculed.

[4] The only foundation for the statement, frequently made, that Geronimo was a medicine man. (SMB)

But numerous other accounts suggest that Geronimo was a "medicine man" and that his powers of divination and healing made him feared and perhaps even disliked by not a few of his own people. I have called him a war shaman in my Introduction. (FT)

4

TRIBAL AMUSEMENTS, MANNERS, AND CUSTOMS

To celebrate each noted event a feast and dance would be given. Perhaps only our own people, perhaps neighboring tribes, would be invited. These festivities usually lasted for about four days. By day we feasted, by night under the direction of some chief we danced. The music for our dance was singing led by the warriors, and accompanied by beating the esadadedne (buckskin-on-a-hoop). No words were sung —only the tones. When the feasting and dancing were over we would have horse races, foot races, wrestling, jumping, and all sorts of games (gambling).

Among these games the most noted was the tribal game of Kah (foot). It is played as follows: Four moccasins are placed about four feet apart in holes in the ground, dug in a row on one side of the camp, and on the opposite side a similar parallel row. At night a camp fire is started between these two rows of moccasins, and the players are arranged on sides, one or any number on each side. The score is kept by a bundle of sticks, from which each side takes a stick for every point won. First one side takes the bone,[1] puts up blankets between the four moccasins and the fire so that the opposing team cannot observe their movements, and then begin to sing the legends of creation. The side having the bone represents the feathered tribe, the opposite side represents the beasts. The players representing the birds do all the singing, and while singing hide the bone in one of the moccasins, then the blankets are thrown down. They continue to sing, but as soon as the blankets are thrown down the chosen player from the opposing team, armed with a war club, comes to their side of the camp fire and with his club strikes the moccasin in which he thinks the bone is hidden. If he strikes the right moccasin, his side gets the bone, and in turn represents the birds, while the opposing team must keep quiet and guess in turn. There are only four plays; three that lose and one that wins. When all the sticks are gone from the bundle the side having the largest number of sticks is counted winner.

This game is seldom played except as a gambling game, but for that purpose it is the most popular game known to the tribe. Usually the game lasts four or five hours. It is never played in daytime.

After the games are all finished the visitors say, "We are satisfied," and the camp is broken up. I was always glad when the dances and feasts were announced. So were all the other young people.

Our life also had a religious side. We had no churches, no religious organizations, no sabbath day, no holidays, and yet we worshiped. Sometimes the whole tribe would assemble to sing and pray; sometimes a smaller number, perhaps only two or three. The songs had a few words, but were not for-

---

[1] A symbol of the white rock used by the eagle in slaying the nameless monster—see Chapter I. (SMB)

mal. The singer would occasionally put in such words as he wished instead of the usual tone sound. Sometimes we prayed in silence; sometimes each one prayed aloud; sometimes an aged person prayed for all of us. At other times one would rise and speak to us of our duties[2] to each other and to Usen. Our services were short.

When disease or pestilence abounded we were assembled and questioned by our leaders to ascertain what evil we had done, and how Usen could be satisfied. Sometimes sacrifice was deemed necessary. Sometimes the offending one was punished.

If an Apache had allowed his aged parents to suffer for food or shelter, if he had neglected or abused the sick, if he had profaned our religion, or had been unfaithful, he might be banished from the tribe.

The Apaches had no prisons as white men have. Instead of sending their criminals into prison they sent them out of their tribe. These faithless, cruel, lazy, or cowardly members of the tribe were excluded in such a manner that they could not join any other tribe. Neither could they have any protection from our unwritten tribal laws. Frequently these outlaw Indians banded together and committed depredations which were charged against the regular tribe. However, the life of an outlaw Indian was a hard lot, and their bands never became very large; besides, these bands frequently provoked the wrath of the tribe and secured their own destruction.

When I was about eight or ten years old I began to follow the chase, and to me this was never work.

Out on the prairies, which ran up to our mountain

[2] The Apaches recognized no duties to any man outside their tribe. It was no sin to kill enemies or to rob them. However, if they accepted any favor from a stranger, or allowed him to share their comforts in any way, he became (by adoption) related to the tribe and they must recognize their duty to him. (SMB)

Frank Randall took this photograph of an Apache family on the San Carlos Reservation in 1884 at the same time that he took the famous photograph of Geronimo kneeling with a rifle. Compare the wickiups shown here with those in view at the hostiles' camp at Cañon de los Embudos (page 184), some two years later. (COURTESY OF THE NATIONAL ARCHIVES AND RECORDS SERVICE)

homes, wandered herds of deer, antelope, elk, and buffalo, to be slaughtered when we needed them.

Usually we hunted buffalo on horseback, killing them with arrows and spears. Their skins were used to make tepees and bedding; their flesh, to eat.

It required more skill to hunt the deer than any other animal. We never tried to approach a deer except against the wind. Frequently we would spend hours in stealing upon grazing deer. If they were in the open we would crawl long distances on the ground, keeping a weed or brush before us, so that our approach would not be noticed. Often we could kill several out of one herd before the others would run away. Their flesh was dried and packed in vessels, and would keep in this condition for many months. The hide of the deer was soaked in water and ashes and the hair removed, and then the process of tanning continued until the buckskin was soft and pliable. Perhaps no other animal was more valuable to us than the deer.

In the forests and along the streams were many wild turkeys. These we would drive to the plains, then slowly ride up toward them until they were almost tired out. When they began to drop and hide we would ride in upon them and by swinging from the side of our horses, catch them. If one started to fly we would ride swiftly under him and kill him with a short stick, or hunting club. In this way we could usually get as many wild turkeys as we could carry home on a horse.

There were many rabbits in our range, and we also hunted them on horseback. Our horses were trained to follow the rabbit at full speed, and as they approached them we would swing from one side of the horse and strike the rabbit with our hunting club. If he was too far away we would throw the stick and kill him. This was great sport when we were boys, but as warriors we seldom hunted small game.

There were many fish in the streams, but as we did not eat them, we did not try to catch or kill them. Small boys sometimes threw stones at them or shot at them for practice with their bows and arrows. Usen did not intend snakes, frogs, or fishes to be eaten. I have never eaten of them.[3]

There were many eagles in the mountains. These we hunted for their feathers. It required great skill to steal upon an eagle, for besides having sharp eyes, he is wise and never stops at any place where he does not have a good view of the surrounding country.

I have killed many bears with a spear, but was never injured in a fight with one. I have killed several mountain lions with arrows, and one with a spear. Both bears and mountain lions are good for food and valuable for their skin.[4] When we killed them we carried them home on our horses. We often made quivers for our arrows from the skin of the mountain lion. These were very pretty and very durable.

During my minority we had never seen a missionary or a priest. We had never seen a white man. Thus quietly lived the Be-don-ko-he Apaches.

[3] This is not idiosyncratic on Geronimo's part, but a cultural taboo. Reptiles were not acceptable food nor were other creatures which were believed to eat them. (FT)
[4] There is probably an error here, either in translation or transmission: the Chiricahuas had a taboo against eating bear meat. (FT)

5

THE FAMILY

My grandfather, Maco, had been our chief. I never saw him, but my father often told me of the great size, strength, and sagacity of this old warrior. Their principal wars had been with the Mexicans. They had some wars with other tribes of Indians also, but were seldom at peace for any great length of time with the Mexican towns.

Maco died when my father was but a young warrior, and Mangus-Colorado[1] became chief of the Bedonkohe Apaches. When I was but a small boy my father died, after having been sick for some time. When he passed away, carefully the watchers closed his eyes, then they arrayed him in his best

[1] Maco was chief of the Nedni Apaches. His son (Geronimo's father) had married a Bedonkohe Apache (Geronimo's mother) and joined her tribe, thereby losing his right to rule by heredity. By this it will be seen Geronimo could not become chief by hereditary right, although his grandfather was a chieftain. It is also shown that Geronimo's father could not be chief, hence the accession of Mangus-Colorado. (SMB)

Most authorities believe Barrett was incorrect in identifying Maco or Mahko as a Nedni; he apparently was a Bedonkohe. (FT)

clothes, painted his face afresh, wrapped a rich blanket around him, saddled his favorite horse, bore his arms in front of him, and led his horse behind, repeating in wailing tones his deeds of valor as they carried his body to a cave in the mountain. Then they slew his horses, and we gave away all of his other property, as was customary in our tribe, after which his body was deposited in the cave, his arms beside him.[2] His grave is hidden by piles of stone. Wrapped in splendor he lies in seclusion, and the winds in the pines sing a low requiem over the dead warrior.

After my father's death I assumed the care of my mother. She never married again, although according to the customs of our tribe she might have done so immediately after his death. Usually, however, the widow who has children remains single after her husband's death for two or three years; but the widow without children marries again immediately. After a warrior's death his widow returns to her people and may be given away or sold by her father or brothers. My mother chose to live with me, and she never desired to marry again. We lived near our old home and I supported her.

In 1846, being seventeen years of age, I was admitted to the council of the warriors. Then I was very happy, for I could go wherever I wanted and do whatever I liked. I had not been under the control of any individual, but the customs of our tribe prohibited me from sharing the glories of the warpath until the council admitted me. When opportunity offered, after this, I could go on the warpath with my tribe.

---

[2] The Apaches will not keep any of the property of a deceased relative. Their unwritten tribal laws forbid it, because they think that otherwise the children or other relatives of one who had much property might be glad when their father or relatives died. (SMB)

It should also be noted that such practices manifest the profound Chiricahua fear of ghosts. (FT)

This would be glorious. I hoped soon to serve my people in battle. I had long desired to fight with our warriors.

Perhaps the greatest joy to me was that now I could marry the fair Alope, daughter of No-po-so. She was a slender, delicate girl, but we had been lovers for a long time. So, as soon as the council granted me these privileges I went to see her father concerning our marriage. Perhaps our love was of no interest to him; perhaps he wanted to keep Alope with him, for she was a dutiful daughter; at any rate he asked many ponies for her. I made no reply, but in a few days appeared before his wigwam with the herd of ponies and took with me Alope. This was all the marriage ceremony necessary in our tribe.

Not far from my mother's tepee I had made for us a new home. The tepee was made of buffalo hides and in it were many bear robes, lion hides, and other trophies of the chase, as well as my spears, bows, and arrows. Alope had made many little decorations of beads and drawn work on buckskin, which she placed in our tepee.[3] She also drew many pictures on the walls of our home. She was a good wife, but she was never strong. We followed the traditions of our fathers and were happy. Three children came to us—children that played, loitered, and worked as I had done.

---

[3] Beads were obtained from the Mexicans. The Apaches also got money from the Mexicans, but deemed it of no value, and either gave it to their children to play with or threw it away. (SMB)

PART II

THE MEXICANS

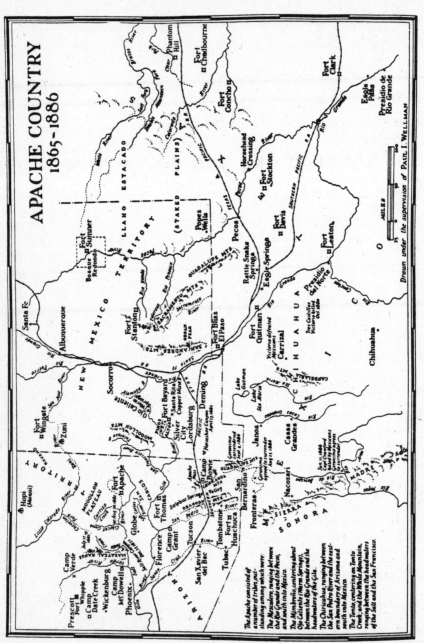

Map of "Apache Country" (COURTESY ATLAS OF AMERICAN HISTORY)

6

KAS-KI-YEH

PART I—THE MASSACRE
In the summer of 1858, being at peace with the Mexican towns as well as with all the neighboring Indian tribes, we went south into Old Mexico to trade.[1] Our whole tribe (Bedonkohe Apaches) went through Sonora toward Casa Grande, our destination, but just before reaching that place we stopped at another Mexican town called by the Indians "Kas-ki-yeh." Here we stayed for several days, camping just outside the city. Every day we would go into town to trade, leaving our camp under the protection of a small guard so that our arms, supplies, and women and children would not be disturbed during our absence.

[1] Most of these dates should be taken as approximations, but this should not lead the reader (as it has led many) to assume that *all* details are highly fictionalized because the Chiricahuas kept no written records. A nonliterate people of necessity develops habits of mind which give rise to incredible feats of memory such as those mentioned in so many of the early missionary accounts of American Indians. The whole history and customs of a tribe exist only in memory, and this is therefore a highly prized mental attribute. (FT)

Late one afternoon when returning from town we were met by a few women and children who told us that Mexican troops from some other town had attacked our camp, killed all the warriors of the guard, captured all our ponies, secured our arms, destroyed our supplies, and killed many of our women and children.[2] Quickly we separated, concealing ourselves as best we could until nightfall, when we assembled at our appointed place of rendezvous—a thicket by the river. Silently we stole in one by one: sentinels were placed, and, when all were counted, I found that my aged mother, my young wife, and my three small children were among the slain. There were no lights in camp, so without being noticed I silently turned away and stood by the river. How long I stood there I do not know, but when I saw the warriors arranging for a council I took my place.

That night I did not give my vote for or against any measure; but it was decided that as there were only eighty warriors left, and as we were without arms or supplies, and were furthermore surrounded by the Mexicans far inside their own territory, we could not hope to fight successfully. So our chief, Mangus-Colorado, gave the order to start at once in perfect silence for our homes in Arizona, leaving the dead upon the field.

I stood until all had passed, hardly knowing what I would do—I had no weapon, nor did I hardly wish to fight, neither did I contemplate recovering the bodies of my loved ones, for that was forbidden. I did not pray, nor did I resolve to do anything in particular, for I had no purpose left. I finally fol-

[2] Such an incident was typical of Chiricahua-Mexican relations: when one party acted in peace the other acted in treachery. Here we have illustrated the classic Mexican ploy of trading while preparing a surprise attack. Often the male Chiricahuas were beguiled by drink and then either executed or enslaved for use in northern Mexico or on the chicle plantations in the Yucatán. (FT)

lowed the tribe silently, keeping just within hearing distance of the soft noise of the feet of the retreating Apaches.

The next morning some of the Indians killed a small amount of game and we halted long enough for the tribe to cook and eat, when the march was resumed. I had killed no game, and did not eat. During the first march as well as while we were camped at this place I spoke to no one and no one spoke to me—there was nothing to say.[3]

For two days and three nights we were on forced marches, stopping only for meals; then we made a camp near the Mexican border, where we rested two days. Here I took some food and talked with the other Indians who had lost in the massacre, but none had lost as I had, for I had lost all.

Within a few days we arrived at our own settlement. There were the decorations that Alope had made—and there were the playthings of our little ones. I burned them all, even our tepee.[4] I also burned my mother's tepee and destroyed all her property.

I was never again contented in our quiet home. True, I could visit my father's grave, but I had vowed vengeance upon the Mexican troopers who had wronged me, and whenever I came near his grave or saw anything to remind me of former happy days my heart would ache for revenge upon Mexico.

PART II—REVENGE

As soon as we had again collected some arms and supplies Mangus-Colorado, our chief, called a council and found that

[3] The Chiricahuas considered emotional demonstrativeness unbecoming since anything deeply felt could be translated into actions. (FT)
[4] According to custom he should not have kept the property of his deceased relatives, but he was not compelled to destroy his own tepee or the playthings of his children. (SMB)

all our warriors were willing to take the warpath against Mexico. I was appointed to solicit the aid of other tribes in this war.

When I went to the Chokonen (Chiricahua) Apaches, Cochise, their chief, called a council at early dawn. Silently the warriors assembled at an open place in a mountain dell and took their seats on the ground, arranged in rows according to their ranks. Silently they sat smoking. At a signal from the chief I arose and presented my cause as follows:

"Kinsman, you have heard what the Mexicans have recently done without cause. You are my relatives—uncles, cousins, brothers. We are men the same as the Mexicans are —we can do to them what they have done to us. Let us go forward and trail them—I will lead you to their city—we will attack them in their homes. I will fight in the front of the battle—I only ask you to follow me to avenge this wrong done by these Mexicans—will you come? It is well—you will all come.

"Remember the rule in war—men may return or they may be killed. If any of these young men are killed I want no blame from their kinsmen, for they themselves have chosen to go. If I am killed no one need mourn for me. My people have all been killed in that country, and I, too, will die if need be."

I returned to my own settlement, reported this success to my chieftain, and immediately departed to the southward into the land of the Nedni Apaches. Their chief, Whoa, heard me without comment, but he immediately issued orders for a council, and when all were ready gave a sign that I might speak. I addressed them as I had addressed the Chokonen tribe, and they also promised to help us.

It was in the summer of 1859, almost a year from the date of the massacre of Kaskiyeh, that these three tribes were assembled on the Mexican border to go upon the warpath. Their faces were painted, the war bands[5] fastened upon their brows, their long scalp-locks[6] ready for the hand and knife of the warrior who would overcome them. Their families had been hidden away in a mountain rendezvous near the Mexican border. With these families a guard was posted, and a number of places of rendezvous designated in case the camp should be disturbed.

When all were ready the chieftains gave command to go forward. None of us were mounted and each warrior wore moccasins and also a cloth wrapped about his loins. This cloth could be spread over him when he slept, and when on the march would be ample protection as clothing. In battle, if the fight was hard, we did not wish much clothing. Each warrior carried three days' rations, but as we often killed game while on the march, we seldom were without food.

We traveled in three divisions: the Bedonkohe Apaches led by Mangus-Colorado, the Chokonen Apaches by Cochise, and the Nedni Apaches by Whoa; however, there was no regular order inside the separate tribes. We usually marched about fourteen hours per day, making three stops for meals, and traveling forty to forty-five miles a day.

I acted as guide into Mexico, and we followed the river courses and mountain ranges because we could better thereby keep our movements concealed. We entered Sonora and went southward past Quitaro, Nacozari, and many smaller settlements.

When we were almost at Arispe we camped, and eight men rode out from the city to parley with us. These we

[5] Strips of buckskin about two inches wide fastened around the head. (SMB)
[6] At this time the Mexican Government offered a reward in gold for Apache scalps—one hundred dollars for warrior's scalp, fifty dollars for squaw's scalp, and twenty-five dollars for child's scalp. (SMB)

Chief Naiche, son of Cochise, with his wife Ha-o-zinne. Said to bear a strong physical resemblance to his almost-legendary father, Naiche apparently lacked some of Cochise's fire and military skills. However, conditions had changed greatly since Cochise's time. In any event, in the last of the prereservation days, the chief appears almost in the role of Geronimo's lieutenant. *(COURTESY OF THE SMITHSONIAN INSTITUTION: NATIONAL ANTHROPOLOGICAL ARCHIVES)*

captured, killed, and scalped. This was to draw the troops from the city, and the next day they came. The skirmishing lasted all day without a general engagement, but just at night we captured their supply train, so we had plenty of provisions and some more guns.

That night we posted sentinels and did not move our camp, but rested quietly all night, for we expected heavy work the next day. Early the next morning the warriors were assembled to pray—not for help, but that they might have health and avoid ambush or deceptions by the enemy.

As we had anticipated, about ten o'clock in the morning the whole Mexican force came out. There were two companies of cavalry and two of infantry. I recognized the cavalry as the soldiers who had killed my people at Kaskiyeh. This I told to the chieftains, and they said that I might direct the battle.

I was no chief and never had been, but because I had been more deeply wronged than others, this honor was conferred upon me, and I resolved to prove worthy of the trust. I arranged the Indians in a hollow circle near the river, and the Mexicans drew their infantry up in two lines, with the cavalry in reserve. We were in the timber, and they advanced until within about four hundred yards, when they halted and opened fire. Soon I led a charge against them, at the same time sending some braves to attack their rear. In all the battle I thought of my murdered mother, wife, and babies—of my father's grave and my vow of vengeance, and I fought with fury. Many fell by my hand, and constantly I led the advance. Many braves were killed. The battle lasted about two hours.

At the last four Indians were alone in the center of the field—myself and three other warriors. Our arrows were all gone, our spears broken off in the bodies of dead enemies. We had only our hands and knives with which to fight, but all who had stood against us were dead. Then two armed soldiers came upon us from another part of the field. They shot down two of our men and we, the remaining two, fled toward our own warriors. My companion was struck down by a saber, but I reached our warriors, seized a spear, and turned. The one who pursued me missed his aim and fell by my spear. With his saber I met the trooper who had killed my companion and we grappled and fell. I killed him with my knife and quickly rose over his body, brandishing his saber, seeking for other troopers to kill. There were none. But the Apaches had seen.[7] Over the bloody field, covered with the bodies of Mexicans, rang the fierce Apache war-whoop.

Still covered with the blood of my enemies, still holding my conquering weapon, still hot with the joy of battle, victory, and vengeance, I was surrounded by the Apache braves and made war chief of all the Apaches. Then I gave orders for scalping the slain.[8]

I could not call back my loved ones, I could not bring back the dead Apaches, but I could rejoice in this revenge. The Apaches had avenged the massacre of "Kas-ki-yeh."

[7] It was by such feats of battle that Geronimo rose to leadership. Such individual exploits became part of a man's "record" within the tribe, and he was careful to confine himself to fact in his periodic recital of them; otherwise he might be contradicted and ridiculed by other witnesses. (FT)

[8] From the moment the command for war is given with the Apaches everything assumes a religious guise. The manner of camping, cooking, etc., are exactly prescribed. Every object appertaining to war is called by its sacred name; as if, for instance, in English, one should say not horse, but war-horse or charger; not arrow, but missile of death. The Indian is not called by his ordinary name, but by a sacred name to which is subjoined "brave" or "chief" as the case may be. Geronimo's Indian name was Go khlä yeh, but the Mexicans at this battle called him Geronimo, a name he has borne ever since both among the Indians and white men. (SMB)

Such specialization within the culture (a vocabulary of almost one hundred war-related terms has been collected) tells us much about the old Chiricahua way and its major emphasis. (FT)

7

FIGHTING UNDER DIFFICULTIES

All the other Apaches were satisfied after the battle of "Kaski-yeh," but I still desired more revenge. For several months we were busy with the chase and other peaceful pursuits. Finally I succeeded in persuading two other warriors, Ah-kochne and Ko-deh-ne, to go with me to invade the Mexican country.

We left our families with the tribe and went on the warpath.[1] We were on foot and carried three days' rations. We entered Mexico on the north line of Sonora and followed the Sierra de Antunez Mountains to the south end of the range. Here we decided to attack a small village. (I do not know the name of this village.) At daylight we approached from the

---

[1] Geronimo had married again. (SMB)

Years later a Chiricahua who apparently had read Geronimo's autobiography used this detail to "prove" that it was really Barrett who wrote the book since no Chiricahua would have remarried so soon after the death of his wife unless he married a relative or sister of hers—which Geronimo did not. But no mention is made here of how much time elapsed between the death of the first wife and the marriage to the second. (FT)

mountains. Five horses were hitched outside. We advanced cautiously, but just before we reached the horses the Mexicans opened fire from the houses. My two companions were killed. Mexicans swarmed on every side; some were mounted; some were on foot, and all seemed to be armed. Three times that day I was surrounded, but I kept fighting, dodging, and hiding. Several times during the day while in concealment I had a chance to take deliberate aim at some Mexican, who, gun in hand, was looking for me. I do not think I missed my aim either time. With the gathering darkness I found more time to retreat toward Arizona. But the Mexicans did not quit the chase. Several times the next day mounted Mexicans tried to head me off; many times they fired on me, but I had no more arrows; so I depended upon running and hiding, although I was very tired. I had not eaten since the chase began, nor had I dared to stop for rest. The second night I got clear of my pursuers, but I never slackened my pace until I reached our home in Arizona. I came into our camp without booty, without my companions, exhausted, but not discouraged.

The wives and children of my two dead companions were cared for by their people. Some of the Apaches blamed me for the evil result of the expedition, but I said nothing. Having failed, it was only proper that I should remain silent. But my feelings toward the Mexicans did not change—I still hated them and longed for revenge. I never ceased to plan for their punishment, but it was hard to get the other warriors to listen to my proposed raids.

In a few months after this last adventure I persuaded two other warriors to join me in raiding the Mexican frontier. On our former raid we had gone through the Nedni Apaches' range into Sonora. This time we went through the country of the Cho-kon-en and entered the Sierra Madre Mountains. We traveled south, secured more rations, and prepared to begin our raids. We had selected a village near the mountains which we intended to attack at daylight. While asleep that night Mexican scouts discovered our camp and fired on us, killing one warrior. In the morning we observed a company of Mexican troops coming from the south. They were mounted and carried supplies for a long journey. We followed their trail until we were sure that they were headed for our range in Arizona; then we hurried past them and in three days reached our own settlement. We arrived at noon, and that afternoon, about three o'clock, these Mexican troops attacked our settlement. Their first volley killed three small boys. Many of the warriors of our tribe were away from home, but the few of us who were in camp were able to drive the troops out of the mountains before night. We killed eight Mexicans and lost five—two warriors and three boys. The Mexicans rode due south in full retreat. Four warriors were detailed to follow them, and in three days these trailers returned, saying that the Mexican cavalry had left Arizona, going southward. We were quite sure they would not return soon.

Soon after this (in the summer of 1860) I was again able to take the warpath against the Mexicans, this time with twenty-five warriors. We followed the trail of the Mexican troops last mentioned and entered the Sierra de Sahuaripa Mountains. The second day in these mountains our scouts discovered mounted Mexican troops. There was only one company of cavalry in this command, and I thought that by properly surprising them we could defeat them. We ambushed the trail over which they were to come. This was at a place where the whole company must pass through a mountain defile. We reserved fire until all of the troops had passed through; then the signal was given. The Mexican troopers, seemingly without a word of command, dismounted, and placing their horses on the outside of the company, for breastworks, made a good fight against us. I saw that we could not dislodge them without using all our ammunition, so I led a charge. The warriors suddenly pressed in from all sides and we fought hand to hand. During this encounter I raised my spear to kill a Mexican soldier just as he leveled his gun at me; I was advancing rapidly, and my foot slipping in a pool of blood, I fell under the Mexican trooper. He struck me over the head with the butt of his gun, knocking me senseless. Just at that instant a warrior who followed in my footsteps killed the Mexican with a spear. In a few minutes not a Mexican soldier was left alive. When the Apache war-cry had died away, and their enemies had been scalped, they began to care for their dead and wounded. I was found lying unconscious where I had fallen. They bathed my head in cold water and restored me to consciousness. Then they bound up my wound and the next morning, although weak from loss of blood and suffering from a severe headache, I was able to march on the return to Arizona. I did not fully recover for months, and I still wear the scar given me by that musketeer. In this fight we had lost so heavily that there really was no glory in our victory, and we returned to Arizona. No one seemed to want to go on the warpath again that year.

In the summer (1861) with twelve warriors I again went into Mexico. We entered Chihuahua and followed south on the east side of the Sierra Madre Mountains four days' journey; then crossed over to the Sierra de Sahuaripa range, not far east of Casa Grande. Here we rested one day, and sent out scouts to reconnoiter. They reported pack trains camped five miles west of us. The next morning just at daybreak, as these drivers were starting with their mule pack train, we attacked them. They rode away for their lives, leaving us the booty. The mules were loaded with provisions, most of which we took home. Two mules were loaded with side-meat or bacon;

this we threw away.[2] We started to take these pack trains home, going northward through Sonora, but when near Casita, Mexican troops overtook us. It was at daybreak and we were just finishing our breakfast. We had no idea that we had been pursued or that our enemies were near until they opened fire. At the first volley a bullet struck me a glancing lick just at the lower corner of the left eye and I fell unconscious. All the other Indians fled to cover. The Mexicans, thinking me dead, started in pursuit of the fleeing Indians. In a few moments I regained consciousness and had started at full speed for the woods when another company coming up opened fire on me. Then the soldiers who had been chasing the other Indians turned, and I stood between two hostile companies, but I did not stand long. Bullets whistled in every direction and at close range to me. One inflicted a slight flesh wound on my side, but I kept running, dodging, and fighting, until I got clear of my pursuers. I climbed up a steep cañon, where the cavalry could not follow. The troopers saw me, but did not dismount and try to follow. I think they were wise not to come on.

It had been understood that in case of surprise with this booty, our place of rendezvous should be the Santa Bita Mountains in Arizona. We did not reassemble in Mexico, but traveled separately and in three days we were encamped in our place of rendezvous. From this place we returned home empty-handed. We had not even a partial victory to report. I again returned wounded, but I was not yet discouraged.

---

[2] They had never eaten bacon and did not learn to do so for a long time. Even now they will not eat bacon or pork if they can get other meat. Geronimo positively refuses to eat bacon or pork. (SMB)

This is because the Chiricahuas believed that the wild hogs they knew (peccary) ate reptiles; thus all hogs did so and were taboo. (FT)

Again I was blamed by our people, and again I had no reply.

After our return many of the warriors had gone on a hunt and some of them had gone north to trade for blankets from the Navajo Indians. I remained at home trying to get my wounds healed. One morning just at daybreak, when the squaws were lighting the camp fires to prepare breakfast, three companies of Mexican troops who had surrounded our settlement in the night opened fire. There was no time for fighting. Men, women and children fled for their lives. Many women and children and a few warriors were killed, and four women were captured. My left eye was still swollen shut, but with the other I saw well enough to hit one of the officers with an arrow, and then make good my escape among the rocks. The troopers burned our tepees and took our arms, provisions, ponies, and blankets. Winter was at hand.

There were not more than twenty warriors in camp at this time, and only a few of us had secured weapons during the excitement of the attack. A few warriors followed the trail of the troops as they went back to Mexico with their booty, but were unable to offer battle. It was a long, long time before we were again able to go on the warpath against the Mexicans.

The four women who were captured at this time by the Mexicans were taken into Sonora, Mexico, where they were compelled to work for the Mexicans. After some years they escaped to the mountains and started to find our tribe. They had knives which they had stolen from the Mexicans, but they had no other weapons. They had no blankets; so at night they would make a little tepee by cutting brush with their knives, and setting them up for the walls. The top was covered over with brush. In this temporary tepee they would all sleep. One night when their camp fire was low they heard growling just outside the tepee. Francisco, the youngest woman of the party (about seventeen years of age), started to build up the fire, when a mountain lion crashed through the tepee and attacked her. The suddenness of the attack made her drop her knife, but she fought as best she could with her hand. She was no match for the lion, however; her left shoulder was crushed and partly torn away. The lion kept trying to catch her by the throat; this she prevented with her hands for a long time. He dragged her for about 300 yards, then she found her strength was failing her from loss of blood, and she called to the other women for help. The lion had been dragging her by one foot, and she had been catching hold of his legs, and of the rocks and underbrush, to delay him. Finally he stopped and stood over her. She again called her companions and they attacked him with their knives and killed him. Then they dressed her wounds and nursed her in the mountains for about a month. When she was again able to walk they resumed their journey and reached our tribe in safety.

This woman (Francisco) was held as a prisoner of war with the other Apaches and died on the Fort Sill Reservation in 1892. Her face was always disfigured with those scars and she never regained perfect use of her hands. The three older women died before we became prisoners of war.

Many women and children were carried away at different times by Mexicans. Not many of them ever returned, and those who did underwent many hardships in order to be again united with their people. Those who did not escape were slaves to the Mexicans, or perhaps even more degraded.

When warriors were captured by the Mexicans they were kept in chains. Four warriors who were captured once at a place north of Casa Grande, called by the Indians "Honas," were kept in chains for a year and a half, when they were exchanged for Mexicans whom we had captured.

We never chained prisoners or kept them in confinement, but they seldom got away. Mexican men when captured were compelled to cut wood and herd horses. Mexican women and children were treated as our own people.[3]

<hr/>

[3] The interpreter Asa, son of Whoa, remembers a little captive Mexican girl who used to play with the Apache children, but was finally exchanged.

One of Geronimo's wives and her child were killed at this time, and thenceforth until he became a prisoner of war he had two wives. He might have had as many wives as he wished, but he says that he was so busy fighting Mexicans that he could not support more than two. (SMB)

8

RAIDS THAT WERE SUCCESSFUL

In the summer of 1862 I took eight men and invaded Mexican territory. We went south on the west side of the Sierra Madre Mountains for five days; then in the night crossed over to the southern part of the Sierra de Sahuaripa range. Here we again camped to watch for pack trains. About ten o'clock next morning four drivers, mounted, came past our camp with a pack-mule train. As soon as they saw us they rode for their lives, leaving us the booty. This was a long train, and packed with blankets, calico, saddles, tinware, and loaf sugar. We hurried home as fast as we could with these provisions, and on our return while passing through a cañon in the Santa Catalina range of mountains in Arizona, met a white man driving a mule pack train. When we first saw him he had already seen us, and was riding at full tilt up the cañon. We examined his train and found that his mules were all loaded with cheese. We put them in with the other train and resumed our journey. We did not attempt to trail the driver and I am sure he did not try to follow us.

In two days we arrived at home. Then Mangus-Colorado,

our chief, assembled the tribe. We gave a feast, divided the spoils, and danced all night. Some of the pack mules were killed and eaten.

This time after our return we kept out scouts so that we would know if Mexican troops should attempt to follow us.

On the third day our scouts came into camp and reported Mexican cavalry dismounted and approaching our settlement. All our warriors were in camp. Mangus-Colorado took command of one division and I of the other. We hoped to get possession of their horses, then surround the troops in the mountains, and destroy the whole company. This we were unable to do, for they, too, had scouts. However, within four hours after we started we had killed ten troopers with the loss of only one man, and the Mexican cavalry was in full retreat, followed by thirty armed Apaches, who gave them no rest until they were far inside the Mexican country. No more troops came that winter.

For a long time we had plenty of provisions, plenty of blankets, and plenty of clothing. We also had plenty of cheese and sugar.

Another summer (1863) I selected three warriors and went on a raid into Mexico. We went south into Sonora, camping in the Sierra de Sahuaripa Mountains. About forty miles west of Casa Grande is a small village in the mountains, called by the Indians "Crassanas." We camped near this place and concluded to make an attack. We had noticed that just at midday no one seemed to be stirring; so we planned to make our attack at the noon hour. The next day we stole into the town at noon. We had no guns, but were armed with spears and bows and arrows. When the war-whoop was given to open the attack the Mexicans fled in every direction; not one of them made any attempt to fight us.

We shot some arrows at the retreating Mexicans, but

Geronimo with three of his warriors at Cañon de los Embudos. Crook noted that the band was well armed, in superb fighting condition, and "as fierce as so many tigers." From the left: Yahnozha, Chappo, Fun, and Geronimo. (COURTESY OF THE FORT SILL MUSEUM, FORT SILL, OKLAHOMA)

killed only one. Soon all was silent in the town and no Mexicans could be seen.

When we discovered that all the Mexicans were gone we looked through their houses and saw many curious things. These Mexicans kept many more kinds of property than the Apaches did. Many of the things we saw in the houses we could not understand, but in the stores we saw much that we wanted; so we drove in a herd of horses and mules, and packed as much provisions and supplies as we could on them. Then we formed these animals into a pack train and returned safely to Arizona. The Mexicans did not even trail us.

When we arrived in camp we called the tribe together and feasted all day. We gave presents to everyone. That night the dance began, and it did not cease until noon the next day.

This was perhaps the most successful raid ever made by us into Mexican territory. I do not know the value of the booty, but it was very great, for we had supplies enough to last our whole tribe for a year or more.

In the fall of 1864 twenty warriors were willing to go with me on another raid into Mexico. These were all chosen men, well armed and equipped for battle. As usual we provided for the safety of our families before starting on this raid. Our whole tribe scattered and then reassembled at a camp about forty miles from the former place. In this way it would be hard for the Mexicans to trail them and we would know where to find our families when we returned. Moreover, if any hostile Indians should see this large number of warriors leaving our range they might attack our camp, but if they found no one at the usual place their raid would fail.

We went south through the Chokonen Apaches' range, entered Sonora, Mexico, at a point directly south of Tombstone, Arizona, and went into hiding in the Sierra de Antunez Mountains.

We attacked several settlements in the neighborhood and secured plenty of provisions and supplies. After about three days we attacked and captured a mule pack train at a place called by the Indians "Pontoco." It is situated in the mountains due west, about one day's journey from Arispe.

There were three drivers with this train. One was killed and two escaped. The train was loaded with mescal, which was contained in bottles held in wicker baskets.[1] As soon as we made camp the Indians began to get drunk and fight each other. I, too, drank enough mescal to feel the effect of it, but I was not drunk.[2] I ordered the fighting stopped, but the order was disobeyed. Soon almost a general fight was in progress. I tried to place a guard out around our camp, but all were drunk and refused to serve. I expected an attack from Mexican troops at any moment, and really it was a serious matter for me, for being in command I would be held responsible for any ill luck attending the expedition. Finally the camp became comparatively still, for the Indians were too drunk to walk or even to fight. While they were in this stupor I poured out all the mescal, then I put out all the fires and moved the pack mules to a considerable distance from camp. After this I returned to camp to try to do something for the wounded. I found that only two were dangerously wounded. From the leg of one of these I cut an arrow head, and from the shoulder of another I withdrew a spear point. When all the wounds had been cared for, I myself kept guard till morning. The next day we loaded our wounded on the pack mules and started for Arizona.

The next day we captured some cattle from a herd and

[1] Mescal is a fiery liquor produced in Mexico from several species of Agave. (SMB)
[2] Most sources agree that Geronimo liked his liquor as well as did any of his tribesmen. (FT)

drove them home with us. But it was a very difficult matter to drive cattle when we were on foot. Caring for the wounded and keeping the cattle from escaping made our journey tedious. But we were not trailed, and arrived safely at home with all the booty.

We then gave a feast and dance, and divided the spoils. After the dance we killed all the cattle and dried the meat. We dressed the hides and then the dried meat was packed in between these hides and stored away. All that winter we had plenty of meat. These were the first cattle we ever had. As usual we killed and ate some of the mules. We had little use for mules, and if we could not trade them for something of value, we killed them.

In the summer of 1865, with four warriors, I went again into Mexico. Heretofore we had gone on foot; we were accustomed to fight on foot; besides, we could more easily conceal ourselves when dismounted. But this time we wanted more cattle, and it was hard to drive them when we were on foot. We entered Sonora at a point southwest from Tombstone, Arizona, and followed the Sierra de Antunez Mountains to the southern limit, then crossed the country as far south as the mouth of Yaqui River. Here we saw a great lake extending beyond the limit of sight.[3] Then we turned north, attacked several settlements, and secured plenty of supplies. When we had come back northwest of Arispe we secured about sixty head of cattle, and drove them to our homes in Arizona. We did not go directly home, but camped in different valleys with our cattle. We were not trailed. When we arrived at our camp the tribe was again assembled for feasting and dancing. Presents were given to everybody; then the cattle were killed and the meat dried and packed.

[3] Gulf of California. (SMB)

9

VARYING FORTUNES

In the fall of 1865 with nine other warriors I went into Mexico on foot. We attacked several settlements south of Casa Grande, and collected many horses and mules. We made our way northward with these animals through the mountains. When near Arispe we made camp one evening, and thinking that we were not being trailed, turned loose the whole herd, even those we had been riding. They were in a valley surrounded by steep mountains, and we were camped at the mouth of this valley so that the animals could not leave without coming through our camp. Just as we had begun to eat our supper our scouts came in and announced Mexican troops coming toward our camp. We started for the horses, but troops that our scouts had not seen were on the cliffs above us, and opened fire. We scattered in all directions, and the troops recovered all our booty. In three days we reassembled at our appointed place of rendezvous in the Sierra Madre Mountains in northern Sonora. Mexican troops did not follow us, and we returned to Arizona without any more fighting and with no booty. Again I had nothing to say, but I was anxious for another raid.

Early the next summer (1866) I took thirty mounted warriors and invaded Mexican territory. We went south through Chihuahua as far as Santa Cruz, Sonora, then crossed over the Sierra Madre Mountains, following the river course at the south end of the range. We kept on westward from the Sierra Madre Mountains to the Sierra de Sahuripa Mountains, and followed that range northward. We collected all the horses, mules, and cattle we wanted, and drove them northward through Sonora into Arizona. Mexicans saw us at many times and in many places, but they did not attack us at any time, nor did any troops attempt to follow us. When we arrived at our homes we gave presents to all, and the tribe feasted and danced. During this raid we had killed about fifty Mexicans.

Next year (1867) Mangus-Colorado led eight warriors on a raid into Mexico.[1] I went as a warrior, for I was always glad to fight the Mexicans. We rode south from near Tombstone, Arizona, into Sonora, Mexico. We attacked some cowboys, and after a fight with them, in which two of their number were killed, we drove all their cattle northward. The second day we were driving the cattle, but had no scouts out. When we were not far from Arispe, Mexican troops rode upon us. They were well armed and well mounted, and when we first saw them they were not half a mile away from us. We left the cattle and rode as hard as we could toward the mountains, but they gained on us rapidly. Soon they opened fire, but were so far away from us that we were unable to reach them with our arrows; finally we reached some timber, and, leaving

[1] Either Geronimo is in error here about the date of this raid (or Barrett, if it is he who worked out the chronology), or the leader of this raid was Mangus, son of Mangas-Coloradas; the father had been cruelly tortured and then murdered by the whites in 1863. (FT)

our ponies, fought from cover. Then the Mexicans halted, collected our ponies, and rode away across the plains toward Arispe, driving the cattle with them. We stood and watched them until they disappeared in the distance, and then took up our march for home.

We arrived home in five days with no victory to report, no spoils to divide, and not even the ponies which we had ridden into Mexico. This expedition was considered disgraceful.

The warriors who had been with Mangus-Colorado on this last expedition wanted to return to Mexico. They were not satisfied, besides they felt keenly the taunts of the other warriors. Mangus-Colorado would not lead them back, so I took command and we went on foot, directly toward Arispe in Sonora, and made our camp in the Sierra de Sahuripa Mountains. There were only six of us, but we raided several settlements (at night), captured many horses and mules, and loaded them with provisions, saddles and blankets. Then we turned to Arizona, traveling only at night. When we arrived at our camp we sent out scouts to prevent any surprise by Mexicans, assembled the tribe, feasted, danced, and divided the spoils. Mangus-Colorado would not receive any of this booty, but we did not care. No Mexican troops followed us to Arizona.

About a year after this (1868) Mexican troops rounded up all the horses and mules of the tribe not far from our settlement. No raids had been made into Mexico that year, and we were not expecting any attacks. We were all in camp, having just returned from hunting.

About two o'clock in the afternoon two Mexican scouts were seen near our settlement. We killed these scouts, but the troops got under way with the herd of our horses and mules before we saw them. It was useless to try to overtake them on foot, and our tribe had not a horse left. I took twenty warriors and trailed them. We found the stock at a cattle ranch in Sonora, not far from Nacozari, and attacked the cowboys who had them in charge. We killed two men and lost none. After the fight we drove off our own stock and all of theirs.

We were trailed by nine cowboys. I sent the stock on ahead and with three warriors stayed in the rear to intercept any attacking parties. One night when near the Arizona line we discovered these cowboys on our trail and watched them camp for the night and picket their horses. About midnight we stole into their camp and silently led away all their horses, leaving the cowboys asleep. Then we rode hard and overtook our companions, who always traveled at night instead of in the daytime. We turned these horses in with the herd and fell back to again intercept anyone who might trail us. What these nine cowboys did next morning I do not know, and I have never heard the Mexicans say anything about it; I know they did not follow us, for we were not molested. When we arrived in camp at home there was great rejoicing in the tribe. It was considered a good trick to get the Mexicans' horses and leave them asleep in the mountains.

It was a long time before we again went into Mexico or were disturbed by the Mexicans.

10

HEAVY FIGHTING

About 1873 we were again attacked by Mexican troops in our settlement, but we defeated them. Then we decided to make raids into Mexico. We moved our whole camp, packing all our belongings on mules and horses, went into Mexico and made camp in the mountains near Nacori. In moving our camp in this way we wanted no one to spy on us, and if we passed a Mexican's home we usually killed the inmates. However, if they offered to surrender and made no resistance or trouble in any way, we would take them prisoners. Frequently we would change our place of rendezvous; then we would take with us our prisoners if they were willing to go, but if they were unruly they might be killed. I remember one Mexican in the Sierra Madre Mountains who saw us moving and delayed us for some time. We took the trouble to get him, thinking the plunder of his house would pay us for the delay, but after we had killed him we found nothing in his house worth having. We ranged in these mountains for over a year, raiding the Mexican settlements for our supplies, but not hav-

A C. S. Fly photograph taken during the negotiations with General Crook, March 25–27, 1886. Naiche is mounted on Geronimo's left, and the two are flanked by kinsmen of Geronimo: Perico, left, and Isisnah, right. (*COURTESY OF THE NATIONAL ARCHIVES AND RECORDS SERVICE*)

ing any general engagement with Mexican troops; then we returned to our homes in Arizona. After remaining in Arizona about a year we returned to Mexico, and went into hiding in the Sierra Madre Mountains. Our camp was near Nacori, and we had just organized bands of warriors for raiding the country, when our scouts discovered Mexican troops coming toward our camp to attack us.

BATTLE OF WHITE HILL

The chief of the Nedni Apaches, Whoa, was with me and commanded one division. The warriors were all marched toward the troops and met them at a place about five miles from our camp. We showed ourselves to the soldiers and they quickly rode to the top of a hill and dismounted, placing their horses on the outside for breastworks. It was a round hill, very steep and rocky, and there was no timber on its sides. There were two companies of Mexican cavalry, and we had about sixty warriors. We crept up the hill behind the rocks, and they kept up a constant fire, but I had cautioned our warriors not to expose themselves to the Mexicans.

I knew that the troopers would waste their ammunition. Soon we had killed all their horses, but the soldiers would lie behind these and shoot at us. While we had killed several Mexicans, we had not yet lost a man. However, it was impossible to get very close to them in this way, and I deemed it best to lead a charge against them.

We had been fighting ever since about one o'clock, and about the middle of the afternoon, seeing that we were making no further progress, I gave the sign for the advance. The war-whoop sounded and we leaped forward from every stone over the Mexicans' dead horses, fighting hand to hand. The attack was so sudden that the Mexicans, running first this way and then that, became so confused that in a few minutes we had killed them all. Then we scalped the slain, carried away our dead, and secured all the arms we needed. That night we moved our camp eastward through the Sierra Madre Mountains into Chihuahua. No troops molested us here and after about a year we returned to Arizona.

Almost every year we would live a part of the time in Old Mexico. There were at this time many settlements in Arizona; game was not plentiful, and besides we liked to go down into Old Mexico. Besides, the lands of the Nedni Apaches, our friends and kinsmen, extended far into Mexico. Their Chief, Whoa, was as a brother to me, and we spent much of our time in his territory.

About 1880 we were in camp in the mountains south of Casa Grande, when a company of Mexican troops attacked us. There were twenty-four Mexican soldiers and about forty Indians. The Mexicans surprised us in camp and fired on us, killing two Indians the first volley. I do not know how they were able to find our camp unless they had excellent scouts and our guards were careless, but there they were shooting at us before we knew they were near. We were in the timber, and I gave the order to go forward and fight at close range. We kept behind rocks and trees until we came within ten yards of their line, then we stood up and both sides shot until all the Mexicans were killed. We lost twelve warriors in this battle.

This place was called by the Indians "Sko-la-ta." When we had buried our dead and secured what supplies the Mexicans had, we went northeast. At a place near Nacori Mexican troops attacked us. At this place, called by the Indians "No-kode," there were about eighty warriors, Bedonkohe and Nedni Apaches. There were three companies of Mexican troops. They attacked us in an open field, and we scattered, firing as we ran. They followed us, but we dispersed, and soon were free from their pursuit; then we reassembled in the Sierra Madre Mountains. Here a council was held, and as Mexican troops were coming from many quarters, we disbanded.

In about four months we reassembled at Casa Grande to make a treaty of peace. The chiefs of the town of Casa Grande, and all of the men of Casa Grande, made a treaty with us. We shook hands and promised to be brothers. Then we began to trade, and the Mexicans gave us mescal. Soon nearly all the Indians were drunk. While they were drunk two companies of Mexican troops, from another town, attacked us, killed twenty Indians, and captured many more.[1] We fled in all directions.

---

[1] It is impossible to get Geronimo to understand that these troops served the general government instead of any particular town. He still thinks each town independent and each city a separate tribe. He cannot understand the relation of cities to the general government. (SMB)

11

GERONIMO'S MIGHTIEST BATTLE

After the treachery and massacre of Casa Grande we did not reassemble for a long while, and when we did we returned to Arizona. We remained in Arizona for some time, living in San Carlos Reservation, at a place now called Geronimo. In 1883 we went into Mexico again. We remained in the mountain ranges of Mexico for about fourteen months, and during this time we had many skirmishes with Mexican troops. In 1884 we returned to Arizona to get other Apaches to come with us into Mexico.[1] The Mexicans were gathering troops in the mountains where we had been ranging, and their numbers were so much greater than ours that we could not hope to fight them successfully, and we were tired of being chased about from place to place.

[1] These are references to a break from the reservation in 1881; the bulk of the hostiles returned in May 1883; Geronimo and his group returned to San Carlos in late February or early March 1884. (FT)

In Arizona we had trouble with the United States soldiers and returned to Mexico.[2]

We had lost about fifteen warriors in Arizona, and had gained no recruits. With our reduced number we camped in the mountains north of Arispe. Mexican troops were seen by our scouts in several directions. The United States troops were coming down from the north. We were well armed with guns and supplied with ammunition, but we did not care to be surrounded by the troops of two governments, so we started to move our camp southward.

One night we made camp some distance from the mountains by a stream. There was not much water in the stream, but a deep channel was worn through the prairie, and small trees were beginning to grow here and there along the bank of this stream.

In those days we never camped without placing scouts, for we knew that we were liable to be attacked at any time. The next morning just at daybreak our scouts came in, aroused the camp, and notified us that Mexican troops were approaching. Within five minutes the Mexicans began firing on us. We took to the ditches made by the stream, and had the women and children busy digging these deeper. I gave strict orders to waste no ammunition and keep under cover. We killed many Mexicans that day and in turn lost heavily, for the fight lasted all day. Frequently troops would charge at one point, be repulsed, then rally and charge at another point.

About noon we began to hear them speaking my name with curses. In the afternoon the general came on the field and the fighting became more furious. I gave orders to my

[2] An exceedingly oblique reference to the May 1885 break from the San Carlos Reservation—a break that was the result of an elaborate plan of Geronimo's and that I explain briefly in my Introduction. (FT)

warriors to try to kill all the Mexican officers. About three
o'clock the general called all the officers together at the right
side of the field. The place where they assembled was not
very far from the main stream, and a little ditch ran out close
to where the officers stood. Cautiously I crawled out this ditch
very close to where the council was being held. The general
was an old warrior. The wind was blowing in my direction,
so that I could hear all he said, and I understood most of it.[3]
This is about what he told them: "Officers, yonder in those
ditches is the red devil Geronimo and his hated band. This
must be his last day. Ride on him from both sides of the
ditches; kill men, women, and children; take no prisoners;
dead Indians are what we want. Do not spare your own men;
exterminate this band at any cost; I will post the wounded to
shoot all deserters; go back to your companies and advance."

Just as the command to go forward was given I took deliberate aim at the general and he fell. In an instant the ground
around me was riddled with bullets, but I was untouched.
The Apaches had seen. From all along the ditches arose the
fierce war-cry of my people. The columns wavered an instant
and then swept on; they did not retreat until our fire had
destroyed the front ranks.

After this their fighting was not so fierce, yet they continued to rally and readvance until dark. They also continued
to speak my name with threats and curses. That night before
the firing had ceased a dozen Indians had crawled out of the
ditches and set fire to the long prairie grass behind the Mexican troops. During the confusion that followed we escaped
to the mountains.

This was the last battle that I ever fought with Mexicans.

[3] Geronimo has a fair knowledge of the Spanish language. (SMB)

United States troops were trailing us continually from this time until the treaty was made with General Miles in Skeleton Cañon.[4]

During my many wars with the Mexicans I received eight wounds, as follows: shot in the right leg above the knee, and still carry the bullet; shot through the left forearm; wounded in the right leg below the knee with a saber; wounded on top of the head with the butt of a musket; shot just below the outer corner of the left eye; shot in left side, shot in the back. I have killed many Mexicans; I do not know how many, for frequently I did not count them. Some of them were not worth counting.

It has been a long time since then, but still I have no love for the Mexicans. With me they were always treacherous and malicious. I am old now and shall never go on the warpath again, but if I were young, and followed the warpath, it would lead into Old Mexico.

[4] This was the final surrender of Geronimo and the Chiricahuas; August 1886. (FT)

PART III

THE WHITE MEN

12

COMING OF THE WHITE MEN

About the time of the massacre of "Kaskiyeh" (1858) we heard that some white men were measuring land to the south of us. In company with a number of other warriors I went to visit them. We could not understand them very well, for we had no interpreter, but we made a treaty with them by shaking hands and promising to be brothers. Then we made our camp near their camp, and they came to trade with us. We gave them buckskin, blankets, and ponies in exchange for shirts and provisions. We also brought them game, for which they gave us some money. We did not know the value of this money, but we kept it and later learned from the Navajo Indians that it was very valuable.

Every day they measured land with curious instruments and put down marks which we could not understand. They were good men, and we were sorry when they had gone on into the west. They were not soldiers. These were the first white men I ever saw.

About ten years later some more white men came. These

were all warriors. They made their camp on the Gila River south of Hot Springs. At first they were friendly and we did not dislike them, but they were not as good as those who came first.

After about a year some trouble arose between them and the Indians, and I took the warpath as a warrior, not as a chief.[1] I had not been wronged, but some of my people had been, and I fought with my tribe; for the soldiers and not the Indians were at fault.

Not long after this some of the officers of the United States troops invited our leaders to hold a conference at Apache Pass (Fort Bowie). Just before noon the Indians were shown into a tent and told that they would be given something to eat. When in the tent they were attacked by soldiers. Our chief, Mangus-Colorado, and several other warriors, by cutting through the tent, escaped; but most of the warriors were killed or captured.[2] Among the Bedonkohe Apaches killed at this time were Sanza, Kladetahe, Niyokahe, and

---

[1] As a tribe they would fight under their tribal chief, Mangus-Colorado. If several tribes had been called out, the war chief, Geronimo, would have commanded. (SMB)

Fairly inaccurate: a war leader was a war leader whatever the circumstances. Geronimo's special function appears to have been that of an organizer and director of raids and wars. There *is* some confusion as to what such individuals did in times of peace, and it is this confusion that Barrett reflects here. (FT)

[2] Regarding this attack, Mr. L. C. Hughes, editor of *The Star*, Tucson, Arizona, to whom I was referred by General Miles, writes as follows:

"It appears that Cochise and his tribe had been on the warpath for some time and he with a number of subordinate chiefs was brought into the military camp at Bowie under the promise that a treaty of peace was to be held, when they were taken into a large tent where handcuffs were put upon them. Cochise, seeing this, cut his way through the tent and fled to the mountains; and in less than six hours had surrounded the camp with from three to five hundred warriors; but the soldiers refused to make fight." (SMB)

Barrett's note corrects Geronimo's mistake as to the principals involved in this incident, but it is doubtful if the Apaches returned with three to five hundred warriors. (FT)

Hostile Chiricahuas in 1886, with Geronimo standing at center. From a photograph by C. S. Fly. (COURTESY OF THE FORT SILL MUSEUM, FORT SILL, OKLAHOMA)

Gopi. After this treachery the Indians went back to the mountains and left the fort entirely alone. I do not think that the agent had anything to do with planning this, for he had always treated us well. I believe it was entirely planned by the soldiers.

From the very first the soldiers sent out to our western country, and the officers in charge of them, did not hesitate to wrong the Indians.[3] They never explained to the Government when an Indian was wronged, but always reported the misdeeds of the Indians. Much that was done by mean white men was reported at Washington as the deeds of my people.

The Indians always tried to live peaceably with the white soldiers and settlers. One day during the time that the soldiers were stationed at Apache Pass I made a treaty with the post. This was done by shaking hands and promising to be brothers. Cochise and Mangus-Colorado did likewise. I do not know the name of the officer in command, but this was the first regiment that ever came to Apache Pass. This treaty was made about a year before we were attacked in a tent, as above related. In a few days after the attack at Apache Pass we organized in the mountains and returned to fight the soldiers. There were two tribes—the Bedonkohe and the Chokonen Apaches, both commanded by Cochise. After a few days' skirmishing we attacked a freight train that was coming in with supplies for the Fort. We killed some of the men and captured the others. These prisoners our chief offered to trade for the Indians whom the soldiers had captured at the massacre in the tent. This the officers refused, so we killed our prisoners, disbanded, and went into hiding in the mountains. Of those who took part in this affair I am the only one now living.

---

[3] This sweeping statement is more general than we are willing to concede, yet it may be more nearly true than our own accounts. (SMB)

In a few days troops were sent out to search for us, but as we were disbanded, it was, of course, impossible for them to locate any hostile camp. During the time they were searching for us many of our warriors (who were thought by the soldiers to be peaceable Indians) talked to the officers and men, advising them where they might find the camp they sought, and while they searched we watched them from our hiding places and laughed at their failures.

After this trouble all of the Indians agreed not to be friendly with the white men any more. There was no general engagement, but a long struggle followed. Sometimes we attacked the white men—sometimes they attacked us. First a few Indians would be killed and then a few soldiers. I think the killing was about equal on each side. The number killed in these troubles did not amount to much, but this treachery on the part of the soldiers had angered the Indians and revived memories of other wrongs, so that we never again trusted the United States troops.[4]

---

[4] Geronimo here describes the Cochise wars extending throughout the 1860s and ending at the beginning of the '70s through the efforts of Thomas Jeffords and General O. O. Howard, both men who earned the trust of Cochise. (FT)

13

GREATEST OF WRONGS

Perhaps the greatest wrong ever done to the Indians was the treatment received by our tribe from the United States troops about 1863. The chief of our tribe, Mangus-Colorado, went to make a treaty of peace for our people with the white settlement at Apache Tejo, New Mexico. It had been reported to us that the white men in this settlement were more friendly and more reliable than those in Arizona, that they would live up to their treaties and would not wrong the Indians.

Mangus-Colorado, with three other warriors, went to Apache Tejo and held a council with these citizens and soldiers. They told him that if he would come with his tribe and live near them, they would issue to him, from the Government, blankets, flour, provisions, beef, and all manner of supplies. Our chief promised to return to Apache Tejo within two weeks. When he came back to our settlement he assembled the whole tribe in council. I did not believe that the people at Apache Tejo would do as they said and therefore I opposed the plan, but it was decided that with part of the tribe Mangus-Colorado should return to Apache Tejo and receive an issue of rations and supplies. If they were as represented, and if these white men would keep the treaty faithfully, the remainder of the tribe would join him and we would make our permanent home at Apache Tejo. I was to remain in charge of that portion of the tribe which stayed in Arizona. We gave almost all of our arms and ammunition to the party going to Apache Tejo, so that in case there should be treachery they would be prepared for any surprise. Mangus-Colorado and about half of our people went to New Mexico, happy that now they had found white men who would be kind to them, and with whom they could live in peace and plenty.

No word ever came to us from them. From other sources, however, we heard that they had been treacherously captured and slain. In this dilemma we did not know just exactly what to do, but fearing that the troops who had captured them would attack us, we retreated into the mountains near Apache Pass.

During the weeks that followed the departure of our people we had been in suspense, and failing to provide more supplies, had exhausted all of our store of provisions. This was another reason for moving camp. On this retreat, while passing through the mountains, we discovered four men with a herd of cattle. Two of the men were in front in a buggy and two were behind on horseback. We killed all four, but did not scalp them; they were not warriors. We drove the cattle back into the mountains, made a camp, and began to kill the cattle and pack the meat.

Before we had finished this work we were surprised and attacked by United States troops, who killed in all seven Indians—one warrior, three women, and three children. The Government troops were mounted and so were we, but we were poorly armed, having given most of our weapons to the division of our tribe that had gone to Apache Tejo, so we fought mainly with spears, bows, and arrows. At first I had a spear, a bow, and a few arrows; but in a short time my spear and all my arrows were gone. Once I was surrounded, but by dodging from side to side of my horse as he ran I escaped. It was necessary during this fight for many of the warriors to leave their horses and escape on foot. But my horse was trained to come at call, and as soon as I reached a safe place, if not too closely pursued, I would call him to me.[1] During this fight we scattered in all directions and two days later reassembled at our appointed place of rendezvous, about fifty miles from the scene of this battle.

About ten days later the same United States troops attacked our new camp at sunrise. The fight lasted all day, but our arrows and spears were all gone before ten o'clock, and for the remainder of the day we had only rocks and clubs with which to fight. We could do little damage with these weapons, and at night we moved our camp about four miles back into the mountains where it would be hard for the cavalry to follow us. The next day our scouts, who had been left behind to observe the movements of the soldiers, returned, saying that the troops had gone back toward San Carlos Reservation.

A few days after this we were again attacked by another company of United States troops. Just before this fight we had been joined by a band of Chokonen Indians under Cochise, who took command of both divisions. We were repulsed, and decided to disband.

After we had disbanded our tribe the Bedonkohe Apaches

---

[1] Geronimo often calls his horses to him in Fort Sill Reservation. He gives only one shrill note and they run to him at full speed. (SMB)

reassembled near their old camp vainly waiting for the return of Mangus-Colorado and our kinsmen. No tidings came save that they had all been treacherously slain.[2] Then a council was held, and as it was believed that Mangus-Colorado was dead, I was elected Tribal Chief.

For a long time we had no trouble with anyone. It was more than a year after I had been made Tribal Chief that United States troops surprised and attacked our camp. They killed seven children, five women, and four warriors, captured all our supplies, blankets, horses, and clothing, and destroyed our tepees. We had nothing left; winter was beginning, and it was the coldest winter I ever knew. After the soldiers withdrew I took three warriors and trailed them. Their trail led back toward San Carlos.

[2] Regarding the killing of Mangus-Colorado, L. C. Hughes of the Tucson, Ariz., *Star*, writes as follows: "It was early in the year '63, when General West and his troops were camped near Membras, that he sent Jack Swilling, a scout, to bring in Mangus, who had been on the warpath ever since the time of the incident with Cochise at Bowie. The old chief was always for peace, and gladly accepted the proffer; when he appeared at the camp General West ordered him put into the guard-house, in which there was only a small opening in the rear and but one small window. As the old chief entered he said: 'This is my end. I shall never again hunt over the mountains and through the valleys of my people.' He felt that he was to be assassinated. The guards were given orders to shoot him if he attempted to escape. He lay down and tried to sleep, but during the night, someone threw a large stone which struck him in the breast. He sprang up and in his delirium the guards thought he was attempting escape and several of them shot him; this was the end of Mangus.

"His head was severed from his body by a surgeon, and the brain taken out and weighed. The head measured larger than that of Daniel Webster, and the brain was of corresponding weight. The skull was sent to Washington, and is now on exhibition at the Smithsonian Institution." (SMB)

A reasonably accurate summary of this affair except that the murder appears to have taken place in the open around a campfire and to have been preceded by extended torture of the prisoner. (FT)

14

REMOVALS

While returning from trailing the Government troops we saw two men, a Mexican and a white man, and shot them off their horses. With these two horses we returned and moved our camp. My people were suffering much and it was deemed advisable to go where we could get more provisions. Game was scarce in our range then, and since I had been Tribal Chief I had not asked for rations from the Government, nor did I care to do so, but we did not wish to starve.

We had heard that Chief Victoria of the Chihenne (Oje Caliente) Apaches was holding a council with the white men near Hot Springs in New Mexico, and that he had plenty of provisions. We had always been on friendly terms with this tribe, and Victoria was especially kind to my people. With the help of the two horses we had captured, to carry our sick with us, we went to Hot Springs. We easily found Victoria and his band, and they gave us supplies for the winter. We stayed with them for about a year, and during this stay we had perfect peace. We had not the least trouble with Mexi-

Victorio, a chief of the Warm Springs Apaches, a military genius, and a man described by a fellow tribesman as "the most nearly perfect human being I have ever seen." He was killed in battle by a Mexican force in October 1880. *(COURTESY OF NATIONAL ARCHIVES AND RECORDS SERVICE)*

cans, white men, or Indians. When we had stayed as long as we should, and had again accumulated some supplies, we decided to leave Victoria's band. When I told him that we were going to leave he said that we should have a feast and dance before we separated.

The festivities were held about two miles above Hot Springs, and lasted for four days. There were about four hundred Indians at this celebration. I do not think we ever spent a more pleasant time than upon this occasion. No one ever treated our tribe more kindly than Victoria and his band. We are still proud to say that he and his people were our friends.

When I went to Apache Pass (Fort Bowie) I found General Howard in command, and made a treaty with him.[1] This treaty lasted until long after General Howard had left our country. He always kept his word with us and treated us as brothers. We never had so good a friend among the United States officers as General Howard. We could have lived forever at peace with him. If there is any pure, honest white man in the United States army, that man is General Howard. All the Indians respect him, and even to this day frequently talk of the happy times when General Howard was in command of our Post. After he went away he placed an agent at Apache Pass who issued to us from the Government clothing, rations, and supplies, as General Howard directed.[2] When beef was issued to the Indians I got twelve steers for my tribe, and Cochise got twelve steers for his tribe. Rations were issued about once a month, but if we ran out we only had to ask

[1] General O. O. Howard was not in command, but had been sent by President Grant, in 1872, to make peace with the Apache Indians. The general wrote me from Burlington, Vt., under date of June 12, 1906, that he remembered the treaty, and that he also remembered with much satisfaction subsequently meeting Geronimo. (SMB)
[2] John P. Clum. For an account of his career as Apache agent, see a book by that title written by his son, Woodworth Clum. (FT)

and we were supplied. Now, as prisoners of war in this Reservation, we do not get such good rations.[3]

Out on the prairie away from Apache Pass a man kept a store and saloon. Some time after General Howard went away a band of outlawed Indians killed this man, and took away many of the supplies from his store.[4] On the very next day after this some Indians at the Post were drunk on "tiswin," which they had made from corn. They fought among themselves and four of them were killed. There had been quarrels and feuds among them for some time, and after this trouble we deemed it impossible to keep the different bands together in peace. Therefore we separated, each leader taking his own band. Some of them went to San Carlos and some to Old Mexico, but I took my tribe back to Hot Springs and rejoined Victoria's band.[5]

---

[3] They do not receive full rations now, as they did then. (SMB)

[4] Apparently a reference to the killing of one Rogers and his cook Spence in April 1876, by a band of outlaw Apaches under Skinya. The trouble between the Apaches that resulted from this incident played a part in the decision of Geronimo and others to leave the reservation in June of the same year. (FT)

[5] This is Geronimo's laconic description of his break from the Fort Bowie Reservation in June 1876. In addition to the intratribal conflicts already alluded to, the Chiricahuas were disturbed by the new orders from Washington that all the Apaches were to be concentrated on the San Carlos Reservation. They had understood that the Fort Bowie home would be theirs forever, and both Victorio and Geronimo refused to go to San Carlos with the others. It should be noted that for the next year Geronimo and Victorio used Hot Springs as a raiding base. (FT)

15

IN PRISON AND
ON THE WARPATH

Soon after we arrived in New Mexico two companies of scouts were sent from San Carlos. When they came to Hot Springs they sent word for me and Victoria to come to town. The messengers did not say what they wanted with us, but as they seemed friendly we thought they wanted a council, and rode in to meet the officers. As soon as we arrived in town soldiers met us, disarmed us, and took us both to headquarters, where we were tried by courtmartial. They asked us only a few questions and then Victoria was released and I was sentenced to the guardhouse. Scouts conducted me to the guardhouse and put me in chains. When I asked them why they did this they said it was because I had left Apache Pass.

I do not think that I ever belonged to those soldiers at Apache Pass, or that I should have asked them where I might go. Our bands could no longer live in peace together, and so we had quietly withdrawn, expecting to live with Victoria's band, where we thought we would not be molested. They also sentenced seven other Apaches to chains in the guard-house.

I do not know why this was done, for these Indians had simply followed me from Apache Pass to Hot Springs. If it was wrong (and I do not think it was wrong) for us to go to Hot Springs, I alone was to blame. They asked the soldiers in charge why they were imprisoned and chained, but received no answer.

I was kept a prisoner for four months, during which time I was transferred to San Carlos. Then I think I had another trial, although I was not present. In fact I do not know that I had another trial, but I was told that I had, and at any rate I was released.

After this we had no more trouble with the soldiers, but I never felt at ease any longer at the Post. We were allowed to live above San Carlos at a place now called Geronimo. A man whom the Indians called "Nick Golee" was agent at this place. All went well here for a period of two years, but we were not satisfied.

In the summer of 1883 a rumor was current that the officers were again planning to imprison our leaders.[1] This rumor served to revive the memory of all our past wrongs—the massacre in the tent at Apache Pass, the fate of Mangus-Colorado, and my own unjust imprisonment, which might easily have been death to me. Just at this time we were told that the officers wanted us to come up the river above Ge-

[1] The chronology is faulty: the break described here took place at the end of September 1881. Geronimo's description of the motivating circumstances, however, sheds new and valuable light on actions assumed to represent simple lawlessness. The Chiricahuas were alarmed by the presence of a large number of troops at San Carlos and by reports (perhaps deliberately circulated by civilians who stood to gain by the flight of the Indians) that they were to be tried for activities in past wars. (FT)

ronimo to a fort (Fort Thomas) to hold a council with them. We did not believe that any good could come of this conference, or that there was any need of it; so we held a council ourselves, and fearing treachery, decided to leave the reservation. We thought it more manly to die on the warpath than to be killed in prison.

There were in all about 250 Indians, chiefly the Bedonkohe and Nedni Apaches, led by myself and Whoa. We went through Apache Pass and just west of there had a fight with the United States troops. In this battle we killed three soldiers and lost none.

We went on toward Old Mexico, but on the second day after this United States soldiers overtook us about three o'clock in the afternoon and we fought until dark. The ground where we were attacked was very rough, which was to our advantage, for the troops were compelled to dismount in order to fight us. I do not know how many soldiers we killed, but we lost only one warrior and three children. We had plenty of guns and ammunition at this time. Many of the guns and much ammunition we had accumulated while living in the reservation, and the remainder we had obtained from the White Mountain Apaches when we left the reservation.

Troops did not follow us any longer, so we went south almost to Casa Grande and camped in the Sierra de Sahuaripa Mountains. We ranged in the mountains of Old Mexico for about a year, then returned to San Carlos, taking with us a herd of cattle and horses.[2]

Soon after we arrived at San Carlos the officer in charge, General Crook, took the horses and cattle away from us. I told him that these were not white men's cattle, but belonged

[2] A highly condensed account of the Apache campaign, 1881–May 1883. For further details see my Introduction and for a firsthand account see Britton Davis, *The Truth about Geronimo*. (FT)

to us, for we had taken them from the Mexicans during our wars. I also told him that we did not intend to kill these animals, but that we wished to keep them and raise stock on our range. He would not listen to me, but took the stock. I went up near Fort Apache and General Crook ordered officers, soldiers, and scouts to see that I was arrested; if I offered resistance they were instructed to kill me.

This information was brought to me by the Indians. When I learned of this proposed action I left for Old Mexico, and about four hundred Indians went with me.[3] They were the Bedonkohe, Chokonen, and Nedni Apaches. At this time Whoa was dead, and Naiche was the only chief with me. We went south into Sonora and camped in the mountains. Troops followed us, but did not attack us until we were camped in the mountains west of Casa Grande. Here we were attacked by Government Indian scouts. One boy was killed and nearly all of our women and children were captured.[4]

After this battle we went south of Casa Grande and made a camp, but within a few days this camp was attacked by Mexican soldiers. We skirmished with them all day, killing a few Mexicans, but sustaining no loss ourselves.

That night we went east into the foothills of the Sierra Madre Mountains and made another camp. Mexican troops trailed us, and after a few days attacked our camp again. This time the Mexicans had a very large army, and we avoided a general engagement. It is senseless to fight when you cannot hope to win.

That night we held a council of war; our scouts had re-

[3] The break of May 17, 1885, which Geronimo engineered and for which he was almost executed by Naiche and Chihuahua when they discovered how he had tricked them. (FT)
[4] Geronimo's whole family, excepting his eldest son, a warrior, were captured. (SMB)

Geronimo and the Chiricahuas in negotiations with General Crook at Cañon de los Embudos, at the end of March 1886. Geronimo is easily recognizable. To his left is the implacably hostile Nana. Crook wears a white pith helmet. To his immediate right is John G. Bourke, whose chronicle of the campaign has been invaluable to historians. *(COURTESY OF ARIZONA HISTORICAL SOCIETY)*

ported bands of United States and Mexican troops at many points in the mountains. We estimated that about two thousand soldiers were ranging these mountains seeking to capture us.

General Crook had come down into Mexico with the United States troops. They were camped in the Sierra de Antunez Mountains. Scouts told me that General Crook wished to see me and I went to his camp. When I arrived General Crook said to me, "Why did you leave the reservation?" I said: "You told me that I might live in the reservation the same as white people lived. One year I raised a crop of corn, and gathered and stored it, and the next year I put in a crop of oats, and when the crop was almost ready to harvest, you told your soldiers to put me in prison, and if I resisted to kill me. If I had been let alone I would now have been in good circumstances, but instead of that you and the Mexicans are hunting me with soldiers." He said: "I never gave any such orders; the troops at Fort Apache, who spread this report, knew that it was untrue." Then I agreed to go back with him to San Carlos.[5]

It was hard for me to believe him at that time. Now I know that what he said was untrue, and I firmly believe that he did issue the orders for me to be put in prison, or to be killed in case I offered resistance.[6]

[5] Geronimo's account of the conference at Cañon de los Embudos, March 25, 27, 1886. The relevant sections of the stenographer's report of this conference are reproduced in Davis, *The Truth about Geronimo*. (FT)
[6] Geronimo's exact words, for which the Editor disclaims any responsibility. (SMB)

16

THE FINAL STRUGGLE

We started with all our tribe to go with General Crook back to the United States, but I feared treachery and decided to remain in Mexico. We were not under any guard at this time. The United States troops marched in front and the Indians followed, and when we became suspicious, we turned back. I do not know how far the United States army went after myself, and some warriors turned back before we were missed, and I do not care.[1]

I have suffered much from such unjust orders as those of General Crook. Such acts have caused much distress to my people. I think that General Crook's death was sent by the Almighty as a punishment for the many evil deeds he committed.

Soon General Miles was made commander of all the west-

---

[1] The figures on the party that bolted into the hills vary. The two most frequently used are: twenty warriors, fourteen women, and two boys; or, nineteen warriors, thirteen women, and six children. (FT)

ern posts, and troops trailed us continually.[2] They were led
by Captain Lawton, who had good scouts. The Mexican soldiers also became more active and more numerous. We had
skirmishes almost every day, and so we finally decided to
break up into small bands. With six men and four women I
made for the range of mountains near Hot Springs, New
Mexico. We passed many cattle ranches, but had no trouble
with the cowboys. We killed cattle to eat whenever we were
in need of food, but we frequently suffered greatly for water.
At one time we had no water for two days and nights and
our horses almost died from thirst. We ranged in the mountains of New Mexico for some time, then thinking that perhaps the troops had left Mexico, we returned. On our return
through Old Mexico we attacked every Mexican found, even
if for no other reason than to kill. We believed they had asked
the United States troops to come down to Mexico to fight
us.

South of Casa Grande, near a place called by the Indians
Gosoda, there was a road leading out from the town. There
was much freighting carried on by the Mexicans over this
road. Where the road ran through a mountain pass we stayed
in hiding, and whenever Mexican freighters passed we killed
them, took what supplies we wanted, and destroyed the remainder. We were reckless of our lives, because we felt that
every man's hand was against us. If we returned to the reservation we would be put in prison and killed; if we stayed
in Mexico they would continue to send soldiers to fight us;
so we gave no quarter to anyone and asked no favors.

After some time we left Gosoda and soon were reunited
with our tribe in the Sierra de Antunez Mountains.

---

[2] As a result of Geronimo's escape, General Crook resigned and was replaced
by General Nelson A. Miles. (FT)

Contrary to our expectations the United States soldiers had not left the mountains in Mexico, and were soon trailing us and skirmishing with us almost every day. Four or five times they surprised our camp. One time they surprised us about nine o'clock in the morning, and captured all our horses (nineteen in number) and secured our store of dried meats.[3] We also lost three Indians in this encounter. About the middle of the afternoon of the same day we attacked them from the rear as they were passing through a prairie—killed one soldier, but lost none ourselves. In this skirmish we recovered all our horses except three that belonged to me. The three horses that we did not recover were the best riding horses we had.

Soon after this we made a treaty with the Mexican troops. They told us that the United States troops were the real cause of these wars, and agreed not to fight any more with us provided we would return to the United States. This we agreed to do, and resumed our march, expecting to try to make a treaty with the United States soldiers and return to Arizona. There seemed to be no other course to pursue.

Soon after this scouts from Captain Lawton's troops told us that he wished to make a treaty with us; but I knew that General Miles was the chief of the American troops, and I decided to treat with him.[4]

---

[3] Captain Lawton reports officially the same engagement (see page 173), but makes no mention of the recapture (by the Apaches) of the horses. (SMB)

[4] Geronimo here describes his initial contact with Lieutenant Charles B. Gatewood, Lawton's advance scout, on August 25, 1886, near Fronteras. The ragged band was finished, militarily speaking, and Geronimo was suffering from the effects of a three-day drunk. He sued for peace on the terms originally offered by Crook in March (immediate reunion with families, a two-year imprisonment in the East, and then return to the reservation), but was refused and was apparently told that return to the reservation was up to Washington. What happened thereafter is a matter much in dispute, as the material collected by Barrett in the Appendix indicates. The clearest reconstruction I can make from

We continued to move our camp northward, and the American troops also moved northward, keeping at no great distance from us, but not attacking us.

I sent my brother Porico (White Horse) with Mr. George Wratton on to Fort Bowie to see General Miles, and to tell him that we wished to return to Arizona; but before these messengers returned I met two Indian scouts—Kayitah, a Chokonen Apache, and Marteen, a Nedni Apache. They were serving as scouts for Captain Lawton's troops. They told me that General Miles had come and had sent them to ask me to meet him. So I went to the camp of the United States troops to meet General Miles.[5]

When I arrived at their camp I went directly to General Miles and told him how I had been wronged, and that I wanted to return to the United States with my people, as we wished to see our families, who had been captured and taken away from us.

General Miles said to me: "The President of the United States has sent me to speak to you. He has heard of your trouble with the white men, and says that if you will agree to a few words of treaty we need have no more trouble. Geronimo, if you will agree to a few words of treaty all will be satisfactorily arranged."

So General Miles told me how we could be brothers to each other. We raised our hands to heaven and said that the treaty was not to be broken. We took an oath not to do any wrong to each other or to scheme against each other.

---

the available evidence is that Geronimo refused Gatewood's surrender proposition and determined to fight it out to the last man; then he changed his mind on the condition that the hostiles would be speedily reunited with their families. This condition was apparently agreed to several days later by General Miles, but it was not fulfilled. (FT)

[5] September 4, 1886. (FT)

Then he talked with me for a long time and told me what he would do for me in the future if I would agree to the treaty. I did not greatly believe General Miles, but because the President of the United States had sent me word I agreed to make the treaty, and to keep it. Then I asked General Miles what the treaty would be. General Miles said to me:[6] "I will take you under Government protection; I will build you a house; I will fence you much land; I will give you cattle, horses, mules, and farming implements. You will be furnished with men to work the farm, for you yourself will not have to work. In the fall I will send you blankets and clothing so that you will not suffer from cold in the winter time.

"There is plenty of timber, water, and grass in the land to which I will send you. You will live with your tribe and with your family. If you agree to this treaty you shall see your family within five days."

I said to General Miles: "All the officers that have been in charge of the Indians have talked that way, and it sounds like a story to me; I hardly believe you."

He said: "This time it is the truth."

I said: "General Miles, I do not know the laws of the white man, nor of this new country where you are to send me, and I might break their laws."

He said: "While I live you will not be arrested."

Then I agreed to make the treaty. (Since I have been a prisoner of war I have been arrested and placed in the guard-house twice for drinking whisky.)

We stood between his troopers and my warriors. We placed a large stone on the blanket before us. Our treaty was made by this stone, and it was to last until the stone should

[6] For terms of treaty see Appendix. (SMB)

136

Geronimo at San Antonio, awaiting his fate. He thought he had surrendered on the field of battle. Now he was given to understand he might be hanged as an outlaw. *(WESTERN HISTORY COLLECTIONS, UNIVERSITY OF OKLAHOMA)*

crumble to dust; so we made the treaty, and bound each other with an oath.

I do not believe that I have ever violated that treaty; but General Miles never fulfilled his promises.[7]

When we had made the treaty General Miles said to me: "My brother, you have in your mind how you are going to kill men, and other thoughts of war; I want you to put that out of your mind, and change your thoughts to peace."

Then I agreed and gave up my arms. I said: "I will quit the warpath and live at peace hereafter."

Then General Miles swept a spot of ground clear with his hand, and said: "Your past deeds shall be wiped out like this and you will start a new life."

---

[7] The criticisms of General Miles in the foregoing chapter are from Geronimo, not from the Editor. (SMB)

17

A PRISONER OF WAR

When I had given up to the Government they put me on the Southern Pacific Railroad and took me to San Antonio, Texas, and held me to be tried by their laws.[1]

In forty days they took me from there to Fort Pickens (Pensacola), Florida. Here they put me to sawing up large logs. There were several other Apache warriors with me, and all of us had to work every day. For nearly two years we were kept at hard labor in this place and we did not see our families until May, 1887. This treatment was in direct violation of our treaty made at Skeleton Cañon.

After this we were sent with our families to Vermont, Alabama, where we stayed five years and worked for the Government. We had no property, and I looked in vain for General Miles to send me to that land of which he had spoken; I

---

[1] Geronimo narrowly escaped civilian trial at San Antonio for murder. The outcome of such a trial at that time and place would have been a foregone conclusion. His deportation to Florida was thus somewhat in the nature of an "escape." (FT)

The Chiricahua prisoners of war on the way to San Antonio and years of captivity in Florida and Alabama. They were under heavy guard, and conditions on the train were subhuman. In the front row, from the left: Fun, Perico, Naiche, Geronimo, Chappo, and Garditha. David Roberts in *Once They Moved like the Wind* says the legendary woman warrior Lozen is third from the right in the back row. *(COURTESY OF THE SMITHSONIAN INSTITUTION: NATIONAL ANTHROPOLOGICAL ARCHIVES)*

longed in vain for the implements, house, and stock that General Miles had promised me.[2]

During this time one of my warriors, Fun, killed himself and his wife. Another one shot his wife and then shot himself. He fell dead, but the woman recovered and is still living.[3]

We were not healthy in this place, for the climate disagreed with us. So many of our people died that I consented to let one of my wives go to the Mescalero Agency in New Mexico to live. This separation is according to our custom equivalent to what the white people call divorce, and so she married again soon after she got to Mescalero. She also kept our two small children, which she had a right to do. The children, Lenna and Robbie, are still living at Mescalero, New Mexico. Lenna is married. I kept one wife, but she is dead now and I have only our daughter Eva with me. Since my separation from Lenna's mother I have never had more than one wife at a time. Since the death of Eva's mother I married another woman (December, 1905) but we could not live happily and separated. She went home to her people—that is an Apache divorce.

Then, as now, Mr. George Wratton superintended the Indians. He has always had trouble with the Indians, because he has mistreated them.[4] One day an Indian, while drunk, stabbed Mr. Wratton with a little knife. The officer in charge took the part of Mr. Wratton and the Indian was sent to prison.

When we first came to Fort Sill, Captain Scott was in

[2] The Chiricahuas were finally transported back to the West in August 1894 —not to their old homelands but to Fort Sill, Oklahoma. (FT)

[3] According to Opler (*An Apache Life-Way*) these two incidents are one and the same. (FT)

[4] In Faulk's *The Geronimo Campaign* there is an episode that illustrates the racist way in which Wratton treated Indians in general and Geronimo in particular. (FT)

Geronimo in a watermelon patch at Fort Sill. At the left is his sixth wife, Ziyah.
(COURTESY OF THE FORT SILL MUSEUM, FORT SILL, OKLAHOMA)

charge, and he had houses built for us by the Government. We were also given, from the Government, cattle, hogs, turkeys and chickens. The Indians did not do much good with the hogs, because they did not understand how to care for them, and not many Indians even at the present time keep hogs. We did better with the turkeys and chickens, but with these we did not have as good luck as white men do. With the cattle we have done very well, indeed, and we like to raise them. We have a few horses also, and have had no bad luck with them.

In the matter of selling our stock and grain there has been much misunderstanding.[5] The Indians understood that the cattle were to be sold and the money given to them, but instead part of the money is given to the Indians and part of it is placed in what the officers call the "Apache Fund." We have had five different officers in charge of the Indians here and they have all ruled very much alike—not consulting the Apaches or even explaining to them. It may be that the Government ordered the officers in charge to put this cattle money into an Apache fund, for once I complained and told Lieutenant Purington that I intended to report to the Government that he had taken some of my part of the cattle money and put it into the Apache Fund, he said he did not care if I did tell.[6]

Several years ago the issue of clothing ceased. This, too,

[5] The Indians are not allowed to sell the cattle themselves. When cattle are ready for market they are sold by the officer in charge, part of the money paid to the Indians who owned them and part of it placed in a general (Apache) fund. The supplies, farming implements, etc., for the Apaches are paid for from this fund. (SMB)

[6] The criticism of Lieutenant Purington is from Geronimo. The Editor disclaims any responsibility for it, as in all cases where individuals are criticized by the old warrior. (SMB)

may have been by the order of the Government, but the Apaches do not understand it.

If there is an Apache Fund, it should some day be turned over to the Indians, or at least they should have an account of it, for it is their earnings.

When General Miles last visited Fort Sill I asked to be relieved from labor on account of my age. I also remembered what General Miles had promised me in the treaty and told him of it. He said I need not work any more except when I wished to, and since that time I have not been detailed to do any work. I have worked a great deal, however, since then, for, although I am old, I like to work and help my people as much as I am able.[7]

---

[7] Geronimo helps make hay and care for the cattle, but does not receive orders from the Superintendent of the Indians. (SMB)

PART IV

THE OLD AND THE NEW

18

UNWRITTEN LAWS
OF THE APACHES

TRIALS

When an Indian has been wronged by a member of his tribe
he may, if he does not wish to settle the difficulty personally,
make complaint to the Chieftain. If he is unable to meet the
offending parties in a personal encounter, and disdains to make
complaint, anyone may in his stead inform the chief of this
conduct, and then it becomes necessary to have an investi-
gation or trial. Both the accused and the accuser are entitled
to witnesses, and their witnesses are not interrupted in any
way by questions, but simply say what they wish to say in
regard to the matter. The witnesses are not placed under oath,
because it is not believed that they will give false testimony
in a matter relating to their own people.

The chief of the tribe presides during these trials, but if it
is a serious offense he asks two or three leaders to sit with
him. These simply determine whether or not the man is
guilty. If he is not guilty the matter is ended, and the com-
plaining party has forfeited his right to take personal ven-

geance, for if he wishes to take vengeance himself, he must object to the trial which would prevent it. If the accused is found guilty the injured party fixes the penalty, which is generally confirmed by the chief and his associates.

ADOPTION OF CHILDREN

If any children are left orphans by the usage of war or otherwise, that is, if both parents are dead, the chief of the tribe may adopt them or give them away as he desires. In the case of outlawed Indians, they may, if they wish, take their children with them, but if they leave the children with the tribe, the chief decides what will be done with them, but no disgrace attaches to the children.

"SALT LAKE"

We obtained our salt from a little lake in the Gila Mountains. This is a very small lake of clear, shallow water, and in the center a small mound arises above the surface of the water. The water is too salty to drink, and the bottom of the lake is covered with a brown crust. When this crust is broken cakes of salt adhere to it. These cakes of salt may be washed clear in the water of this lake, but if washed in other water will dissolve.

When visiting this lake our people were not allowed to even kill game or attack an enemy. All creatures were free to go and come without molestation.

PREPARATION OF A WARRIOR

To be admitted as a warrior a youth must have gone with the warriors of his tribe four separate times on the warpath.

On the first trip he will be given only very inferior food. With this he must be contented without murmuring. On none of the four trips is he allowed to select his food as the warriors do, but must eat such food as he is permitted to have.

On each of these expeditions he acts as servant, cares for the horses, cooks the food, and does whatever duties he should do without being told. He knows what things are to be done, and without waiting to be told is to do them. He is not allowed to speak to any warrior except in answer to questions or when told to speak.

During these four wars he is expected to learn the sacred names of everything used in war, for after the tribe enters upon the warpath no common names are used in referring to anything appertaining to war in any way. War is a solemn religious matter.

If, after four expeditions, all the warriors are satisfied that the youth has been industrious, has not spoken out of order, has been discreet in all things, has shown courage in battle, has borne all hardships uncomplainingly, and has exhibited no color of cowardice, or weakness of any kind, he may by vote of the council be admitted as a warrior; but if any warrior objects to him upon any account he will be subjected to further tests, and if he meets these courageously, his name may again be proposed. When he has proven beyond question that he can bear hardships without complaint, and that he is a stranger to fear, he is admitted to the council of the warriors in the lowest rank. After this there is no formal test for promotions, but by common consent he assumes a station on the battlefield, and if that position is maintained with honor, he is allowed to keep it, and may be asked, or may volunteer, to take a higher station, but no warrior would presume to take a higher station unless he had assurance from the leaders of the tribe that his conduct in the first position was worthy of commendation.

From this point upward the only election by the council in formal assembly is the election of the chief.

Old men are not allowed to lead in battle, but their advice is always respected. Old age means loss of physical power and is fatal to active leadership.

DANCES

All dances are considered religious ceremonies and are presided over by a chief and medicine men. They are of a social or military nature, but never without some sacred characteristic.

A DANCE OF THANKSGIVING

Every summer we would gather the fruit of the yucca, grind and pulverize it and mold it into cakes; then the tribe would be assembled to feast, to sing, and to give praises to Usen. Prayers of Thanksgiving were said by all. When the dance began the leaders bore these cakes and added words of praise occasionally to the usual tone sounds of the music.

THE WAR DANCE

After a council of the warriors had deliberated, and had prepared for the warpath, the dance would be started. In this dance there is the usual singing led by the warriors and accompanied with the beating of the "esadadene," but the dancing is more violent, and yells and war-whoops sometimes almost drown the music. Only warriors participated in this dance.

SCALP DANCE

After a war party has returned, a modification of the war dance is held. The warriors who have brought scalps from the battles exhibit them to the tribe, and when the dance begins these scalps, elevated on poles or spears, are carried around the camp fires while the dance is in progress. During this dance there is still some of the solemnity of the war dance. There are yells and war-whoops, frequently accompanied by discharge of firearms, but there is always more levity than would be permitted at a war dance. After the scalp dance is over the scalps are thrown away. No Apache would keep them, for they are considered defiling.[1]

A SOCIAL DANCE

In the early part of September, 1905, I announced among the Apaches that my daughter, Eva, having attained womanhood, should now put away childish things and assume her station as a young lady. At a dance of the tribe she would make her début, and then, or thereafter, it would be proper for a warrior to seek her hand in marriage. Accordingly, invitations were issued to all Apaches, and many Comanches and Kiowas, to assemble for a grand dance on the green by the south bank of Medicine Creek, near the village of Naiche, former chief of the Chokonen Apaches, on the first night of full moon in September. The festivities were to continue for two days and nights. Nothing was omitted in the preparation that would contribute to the enjoyment of the guests or the perfection of the observance of the religious rite.

To make ready for the dancing the grass on a large circular space was closely mowed.

The singing was led by Chief Naiche, and I, assisted by our medicine men, directed the dance.

First Eva advanced from among the women and danced once around the camp fire; then, accompanied by another young woman, she again advanced and both danced twice

---

[1] This is in keeping with the Chiricahuas' fear of all things connected with death.

Some Chiricahuas claimed that they learned scalping from the Mexicans, and certainly the Mexicans did scalp Apache dead. It has also been claimed that the Apaches scalped *only* Mexicans. (FT)

"The Last of the Bedonkohe Apache Tribe." From the left, Toclanny (actually a Mimbreno Apache and U.S. Army scout), Nahdos-te (sister of Geronimo), Nah-thle-tla (first cousin of Geronimo), and Perico (Porico) or White Horse (second cousin of Geronimo and one of his trusted lieutenants). *(PHOTOGRAPH FROM THE ORIGINAL EDITION. COURTESY OF THE CENTER FOR SOUTHWEST RESEARCH, GENERAL LIBRARY, UNIVERSITY OF NEW MEXICO)*

around the camp fire; then she and two other young ladies advanced and danced three times around the camp fire; the next time she and three other young ladies advanced and danced four times around the camp fire; this ceremony lasted about one hour. Next the medicine men entered, stripped to the waist, their bodies painted fantastically, and danced the sacred dances. They were followed by clown dancers, who amused the audience greatly.

Then the members of the tribe joined hands and danced in a circle around the camp fire for a long time. All the friends of the tribe were asked to take part in this dance, and when it was ended many of the old people retired, and the "lovers' dance" began.

The warriors stood in the middle of the circle and the ladies, two-and-two, danced forward and designated some warrior to dance with them. The dancing was back and forth on a line from the center to the outer edge of the circle. The warrior faced the two ladies, and when they danced forward to the center he danced backward: then they danced backward to the outer edge and he followed facing them. This lasted two or three hours and then the music changed. Immediately the warriors assembled again in the center of the circle, and this time each lady selected a warrior as a partner. The manner of dancing was as before, only two instead of three danced together. During this dance, which continued until daylight, the warrior (if dancing with a maiden) could propose marriage, and if the maiden agreed, he would consult her father soon afterward and make a bargain for her.[2]

Upon all such occasions as this, when the dance is fin-

---

[2] Apache warriors do not go "courting" as our youths do. The associations in the villages afford ample opportunity for acquaintance, and the arranging for marriages is considered a business transaction, but the courtesy of consulting the maiden, although not essential, is considered very polite. (SMB)

ished, each warrior gives a present to the lady who selected him for a partner and danced with him. If she is satisfied with the present he says good-by, if not, the matter is referred to someone in authority (medicine man or chief), who determines the question of what is a proper gift.

For a married lady the value of the present should be two or three dollars; for a maiden the present should have a value of not less than five dollars. Often, however, the maiden receives a very valuable present.

During the "lovers' dance" the medicine men mingle with the dancers to keep out evil spirits.

Perhaps I shall never again have cause to assemble our people to dance, but these social dances in the moonlight have been a large part of our enjoyment in the past, and I think they will not soon be discontinued, at least I hope not.

19

AT THE WORLD'S FAIR

When I was at first asked to attend the St. Louis World's Fair I did not wish to go. Later, when I was told that I would receive good attention and protection, and that the President of the United States said that it would be all right, I consented. I was kept by parties in charge of the Indian Department, who had obtained permission from the President. I stayed in this place for six months. I sold my photographs for twenty-five cents, and was allowed to keep ten cents of this for myself. I also wrote my name for ten, fifteen, or twenty-five cents, as the case might be, and kept all of that money. I often made as much as two dollars a day, and when I returned I had plenty of money—more than I had ever owned before.

Many people in St. Louis invited me to come to their homes, but my keeper always refused.

Every Sunday the President of the Fair sent for me to go to a wild west show. I took part in the roping contests before the audience. There were many other Indian tribes there, and strange people of whom I had never heard.

When people first came to the World's Fair they did nothing but parade up and down the streets. When they got tired of this they would visit the shows. There were many strange things in these shows. The Government sent guards with me when I went, and I was not allowed to go anywhere without them.

In one of the shows some strange men with red caps had some peculiar swords, and they seemed to want to fight.[1] Finally their manager told them they might fight each other. They tried to hit each other over the head with these swords, and I expected both to be wounded or perhaps killed, but neither one was harmed. They would be hard people to kill in a hand-to-hand fight.

In another show there was a strange-looking negro. The manager tied his hands fast, then tied him to a chair. He was securely tied, for I looked myself, and I did not think it was possible for him to get away. Then the manager told him to get loose.

He twisted in his chair for a moment, and then stood up; the ropes were still tied but he was free. I do not understand how this was done. It was certainly a miraculous power, because no man could have released himself by his own efforts.

In another place a man was on a platform speaking to the audience; they set a basket by the side of the platform and covered it with red calico; then a woman came and got into the basket, and a man covered the basket again with the calico; then the man who was speaking to the audience took a long sword and ran it through the basket, each way, and then down through the cloth cover. I heard the sword cut through the woman's body, and the manager himself said she was dead; but when the cloth was lifted from the basket she stepped out,

[1] Turks. (SMB)

Geronimo at the wheel, a "publicity" photograph. *(COURTESY OF THE NATIONAL ARCHIVES AND RECORDS SERVICE)*

smiled, and walked off the stage. I would like to know how she was so quickly healed, and why the wounds did not kill her.

I have never considered bears very intelligent, except in their wild habits, but I had never before seen a white bear. In one of the shows a man had a white bear that was as intelligent as a man. He would do whatever he was told—carry a log on his shoulder, just as a man would; then, when he was told, would put it down again. He did many other things, and seemed to know exactly what his keeper said to him. I am sure that no grizzly bear could be trained to do these things.

One time the guards took me into a little house that had four windows.[2] When we were seated the little house started to move along the ground. Then the guards called my attention to some curious things they had in their pockets. Finally they told me to look out, and when I did so I was scared, for our little house had gone high up in the air, and the people down in the Fair Grounds looked no larger than ants. The men laughed at me for being scared; then they gave me a glass to look through (I often had such glasses which I took from dead officers after battles in Mexico and elsewhere), and I could see rivers, lakes and mountains. But I had never been so high in the air, and I tried to look into the sky. There were no stars, and I could not look at the sun through this glass because the brightness hurt my eyes. Finally I put the glass down, and as they were all laughing at me, I, too, began to laugh. Then they said, "Get out!" and when I looked we were on the street again. After we were safe on the land I watched many of these little houses going up and coming

[2] Ferris wheel. (SMB)

down, but I cannot understand how they travel. They are very curious little houses.

One day we went into another show, and as soon as we were in, it changed into night. It was real night, for I could feel the damp air; soon it began to thunder, and the lightnings flashed; it was real lightning, too, for it struck just above our heads. I dodged and wanted to run away, but I could not tell which way to go in order to get out. The guards motioned me to keep still, and so I stayed. In front of us were some strange little people who came out on the platform; then I looked up again and the clouds were all gone, and I could see the stars shining. The little people on the platform did not seem in earnest about anything they did; so I only laughed at them. All the people around where we sat seemed to be laughing at me.

We went into another place and the manager took us into a little room that was made like a cage; then everything around us seemed to be moving; soon the air looked blue, then there were black clouds moving with the wind. Pretty soon it was clear outside; then we saw a few thin white clouds; then the clouds grew thicker, and it rained and hailed with thunder and lightning. Then the thunder retreated and a rainbow appeared in the distance; then it became dark, the moon rose and thousands of stars came out. Soon the sun came up, and we got out of the little room. This was a good show, but it was so strange and unnatural that I was glad to be on the streets again.

We went into one place where they made glassware. I had always thought that these things were made by hand, but they are not. The man had a curious little instrument, and whenever he would blow through this into a little blaze the glass would take any shape he wanted it to. I am not sure, but I think that if I had this kind of an instrument I could make whatever I wished. There seems to be a charm about it. But I suppose it is very difficult to get these little instruments, or other people would have them. The people in this show were so anxious to buy the things the man made that they kept him so busy he could not sit down all day long. I bought many curious things in there and brought them home with me.

At the end of one of the streets some people were getting into a clumsy canoe, upon a kind of shelf, and sliding down into the water.[3] They seemed to enjoy it, but it looked too fierce for me. If one of these canoes had gone out of its path the people would have been sure to get hurt or killed.

There were some little brown people at the Fair that United States troops captured recently on some islands far away from here.[4]

They did not wear much clothing, and I think that they should not have been allowed to come to the Fair. But they themselves did not seem to know any better. They had some little brass plates, and they tried to play music with these, but I did not think it was music—it was only a rattle. However, they danced to this noise and seemed to think they were giving a fine show.

I do not know how true the report was, but I heard that the President sent them to the Fair so that they could learn some manners, and when they went home teach their people how to dress and how to behave.

I am glad I went to the Fair. I saw many interesting things and learned much of the white people. They are a very kind

[3] Shooting the Chute. (SMB)
[4] Iggorrotes from the Philippines. (SMB)

Geronimo in business at the Louisiana Purchase Exhibition, St. Louis, 1904, with some of the bows and arrows he made for sale there. By this point, the old man understood white American commercialism and, though still a prisoner of war, had become an astute businessman. *(COURTESY OF THE SMITH-SONIAN INSTITUTION: NATIONAL ANTHROPOLOGICAL ARCHIVES)*

and peaceful people.[5] During all the time I was at the Fair no one tried to harm me in any way. Had this been among the Mexicans I am sure I should have been compelled to defend myself often.

I wish all my people could have attended the Fair.[6]

[5] The reader should recall here that Geronimo was not without guile. His statements about white culture often have the appearance of cutting several ways. (FT)
[6] Geronimo was also taken to both the Omaha and the Buffalo Expositions, but during that period of his life he was sullen and took no interest in things. The St. Louis Exposition was held after he had adopted the Christian religion and had begun to try to understand our civilization. (SMB)

20

RELIGION

In our primitive worship only our relations to Usen and the members of our tribe were considered as appertaining to our religious responsibilities.[1] As to the future state, the teachings of our tribe were not specific, that is, we had no definite idea of our relations and surroundings in after life. We believed that there is a life after this one, but no one ever told me as to what part of man lived after death. I have seen many men die; I have seen many human bodies decayed, but I have never seen that part which is called the spirit; I do not know what it is; nor have I yet been able to understand that part of the Christian religion.

We held that the discharge of one's duty would make his future life more pleasant, but whether that future life was

---

[1] The use of the word "primitive" here, a favorite pejorative term of whites to describe other cultures, makes one suspect that either translator Daklugie or Barrett substituted this word for something like "old" or "original." What follows is a faithful depiction of the relatively unorganized state of the Chiricahuas' cosmography. (FT)

worse than this life or better, we did not know, and no one was able to tell us. We hoped that in the future life family and tribal relations would be resumed. In a way we believed this, but we did not know it.

Once when living in San Carlos Reservation an Indian told me that while lying unconscious on the battlefield he had actually been dead, and had passed into the spirit land.

First he came to a mulberry tree growing out from a cave in the ground. Before this cave a guard was stationed, but when he approached without fear the guard let him pass. He descended into the cave, and a little way back the path widened and terminated in a perpendicular rock many hundreds of feet wide and equal in height. There was not much light, but by peering directly beneath him he discovered a pile of sand reaching from the depths below to within twenty feet of the top of the rock where he stood. Holding to a bush, he swung off from the edge of the rock and dropped onto the sand, sliding rapidly down its steep side into the darkness. He landed in a narrow passage running due westward through a cañon which gradually grew lighter and lighter until he could see as well as if it had been daylight; but there was no sun. Finally he came to a section of this passage that was wider for a short distance, and then closing abruptly continued in a narrow path; just where this section narrowed two huge serpents were coiled, and rearing their heads, hissed at him as he approached, but he showed no fear, and as soon as he came close to them they withdrew quietly and let him pass. At the next place, where the passage opened into a wider section, were two grizzly bears prepared to attack him, but when he approached and spoke to them they stood aside and he passed unharmed. He continued to follow the narrow passage, and the third time it widened and two mountain lions crouched in the way, but when he had approached them without fear and had spoken to them they also withdrew. He again entered the narrow passage. For some time he followed this, emerging into a fourth section beyond which he could see nothing: the further walls of this section were clashing together at regular intervals with tremendous sounds, but when he approached them they stood apart until he had passed. After this he seemed to be in a forest, and following the natural draws, which led westward, soon came into a green valley where there were many Indians camped and plenty of game. He said that he saw and recognized many whom he had known in this life, and that he was sorry when he was brought back to consciousness.[2]

I told him if I knew this to be true I would not want to live another day, but by some means, if by my own hands, I would die in order to enjoy these pleasures. I myself have lain unconscious on the battlefield, and while in that condition have had some strange thoughts or experiences; but they are very dim and I cannot recall them well enough to relate them. Many Indians believed this warrior, and I cannot say that he did not tell the truth. I wish I knew that what he said is beyond question true. But perhaps it is as well that we are not certain.

Since my life as a prisoner has begun I have heard the teachings of the white man's religion, and in many respects believe it to be better than the religion of my fathers. However, I have always prayed, and I believe that the Almighty has always protected me.

Believing that in a wise way it is good to go to church,

[2] This dream vision was a standard one among the Chiricahuas and serves to remind us of the various and profound ways in which a culture influences the minds of its people. (FT)

and that associating with Christians would improve my character, I have adopted the Christian religion.[3] I believe that the church has helped me much during the short time I have been a member. I am not ashamed to be a Christian, and I am glad to know that the President of the United States is a Christian, for without the help of the Almighty I do not think he could rightly judge in ruling so many people. I have advised all of my people who are not Christians, to study that religion, because it seems to me the best religion in enabling one to live right.

---

[3] Geronimo joined the Dutch Reformed church and was baptized in the summer of 1903. He attends the services regularly at the Apache Mission, Ft. Sill Military Reservation. (SMB)

Later Geronimo was expelled from the church for incessant gambling. (FT)

21

HOPES FOR THE FUTURE

I am thankful that the President of the United States has given me permission to tell my story. I hope that he and those in authority under him will read my story and judge whether my people have been rightly treated.

There is a great question between the Apaches and the Government. For twenty years we have been held prisoners of war under a treaty which was made with General Miles, on the part of the United States Government, and myself as the representative of the Apaches. That treaty has not at all times been properly observed by the Government, although at the present time it is being more nearly fulfilled on their part than heretofore. In the treaty with General Miles we agreed to go to a place outside of Arizona and learn to live as the white people do. I think that my people are now capable of living in accordance with the laws of the United States, and we would, of course, like to have the liberty to return to that land which is ours by divine right. We are

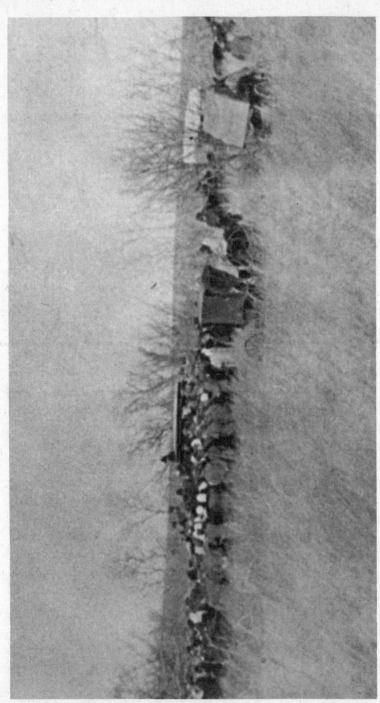

The burial of Geronimo at Fort Sill, February 17, 1909. (COURTESY OF THE FORT SILL MUSEUM, FORT SILL, OKLAHOMA)

reduced in numbers, and having learned how to cultivate the soil would not require so much ground as was formerly necessary. We do not ask all of the land which the Almighty gave us in the beginning, but that we may have sufficient lands there to cultivate. What we do not need we are glad for the white men to cultivate.

We are now held on Comanche and Kiowa lands, which are not suited to our needs—these lands and this climate are suited to the Indians who originally inhabited this country, of course, but our people are decreasing in numbers here, and will continue to decrease unless they are allowed to return to their native land. Such a result is inevitable.

There is no climate or soil which, to my mind, is equal to that of Arizona. We could have plenty of good cultivating land, plenty of grass, plenty of timber and plenty of minerals in that land which the Almighty created for the Apaches. It is my land, my home, my fathers' land, to which I now ask to be allowed to return. I want to spend my last days there, and be buried among those mountains. If this could be I might die in peace, feeling that my people, placed in their native homes, would increase in numbers, rather than diminish as at present, and that our name would not become extinct.

I know that if my people were placed in that mountainous region lying around the headwaters of the Gila River they would live in peace and act according to the will of the President. They would be prosperous and happy in tilling the soil and learning the civilization of the white men, whom they now respect. Could I but see this accomplished, I think I could forget all the wrongs that I have ever received, and die a contented and happy old man. But we can do nothing in this matter ourselves—we must wait until those in authority choose to act. If this cannot be done during my lifetime—if I must die in bondage—I hope that the remnant of the Apache tribe may, when I am gone, be granted the one privilege which they request—to return to Arizona.

Appendix

THE SURRENDER
OF GERONIMO

These materials related to the surrender of Geronimo and the
Chiricahua originally followed Chapter XVI but more properly
belong in an appendix. The reader interested in following further these negotiations should see Britton Davis, *The Truth
about Geronimo*, Odie Faulk, *The Geronimo Campaign*, and Dan L.
Thrapp, *The Conquest of Apacheria*. (FT)

On February 11, 1887, the Senate passed the following
resolution:

"RESOLVED, That the Secretary of War be directed to
communicate to the Senate all dispatches of General Miles
referring to the surrender of Geronimo, and all instructions
given to and correspondence with General Miles in reference
to the same." These papers are published in the Senate Ex-
ecutive Documents, Second Session, 49th Congress, 1886–7,
Volume II, Nos. 111 to 125. For an exhaustive account of
the conditions of Geronimo's surrender the reader is referred
to that document, but this chapter is given to show briefly
the terms of surrender, and corroborate, at least in part, the
statements made by Geronimo.

Upon assuming command of the Department of Arizona,

General Nelson A. Miles was directed by the War Department to use most vigorous operations for the destruction or capture of the hostile Apaches.

The following extracts are from instructions issued April 20th, 1886, for the information and guidance of troops serving in the southern portion of Arizona and New Mexico.

"The chief object of the troops will be to capture or destroy any band of hostile Apache Indians found in this section of the country, and to this end the most vigorous and persistent efforts will be required of all officers and soldiers until the object is accomplished."

.   .   .

"A sufficient number of reliable Indians will be used as auxiliaries to discover any signs of hostile Indians, and as trailers."

.   .   .

"To avoid any advantage the Indians may have by a relay of horses, where a troop or squadron commander is near the hostile Indians he will be justified in dismounting one-half of his command and selecting the lightest and best riders to make pursuit by the most vigorous forced marches until the strength of all the animals of his command shall have been exhausted."

.   .   .

The following telegrams show the efforts of the United States troops and the coöperation of Mexican troops under Governor Torres:

"Headquarters Division of the Pacific,
"Presidio of San Francisco, Cal.
"July 22, 1886.

"ADJUTANT GENERAL,
"Washington, D.C.:

"The following telegram just received from General Miles:

" 'Captain Lawton reports, through Colonel Royall, commanding at Fort Huachuca, that his camp surprised Geronimo's camp on Yongi River, about 130 miles south and east of Campas, Sonora, or nearly 300 miles south of Mexican boundary, capturing all the Indian property, including hundreds of pounds of dried meat and nineteen riding animals. This is the fifth time within three months in which the Indians have been surprised by the troops. While the results have not been decisive, yet it has given encouragement to the troops, and has reduced the numbers and strength of the Indians, and given them a feeling of insecurity even in the remote and almost inaccessible mountains of Old Mexico.'

"In absence of division commander.
"C. MCKEEVER,
"Assistant Adjutant General."

"Headquarters Division of the Pacific,
"Presidio of San Francisco, Cal.
"August 19, 1886.

"ADJUTANT GENERAL,
"Washington, D.C.:

"Following received from General Miles, dated 18th:

" 'Dispatches to-day from Governor Torres, dated Hermosillo, Sonora, Mexico, from Colonels Forsyth and Beaumont, commanding Huachuca and Bowie districts, confirms the following: Geronimo with forty Indians is endeavoring to make terms of peace with Mexican authorities of Fronteraz district. One of our scouts, in returning to Fort Huachuca from Lawton's command, met him, Naiche, and thirteen other Indians on their way to Fronteraz; had a long conversation with them; they said they wanted to make peace, and looked worn and hungry. Geronimo carried his right arm in a sling, bandaged. The splendid work of the troops is evidently having good effect. Should hostiles not surrender to the Mexican authorities, Lawton's command is south of them, and Wilder, with G and M troops, Fourth Cavalry, moved south to Fronteraz, and will be there by 20th. Lieutenant Lockett, with an effective command, will be in good position tomorrow, near Guadalupe Cañon, in Cajon Bonito Mountains. On the 11th I had a very satisfactory interview with Governor Torres. The Mexican officials are acting in concert with ours.'

"O. O. HOWARD,

"Major General."

General O. O. Howard telegraphed from Presidio, San Francisco, California, September 24, 1886, as follows:

". . . The 6th of September General Miles reports the hostile Apaches made overtures of surrender, through Lieutenant Gatewood, to Captain Lawton. They desired certain terms and sent two messengers to me (Miles). They were informed that they must surrender as prisoners of war to troops in the field. They promised to surrender to me in person, and for eleven days Captain Lawton's command moved north, Geronimo and Naiche moving parallel and frequently camping near it. . . . At Skeleton Cañon they halted, saying that they desired to see me (Miles) before surrendering."

After Miles's arrival he reports as follows:

"Geronimo came from his mountain camp amid the rocks and said he was willing to surrender. He was told that they could surrender as prisoners of war; that it was not the way of officers of the Army to kill their enemies who laid down their arms.

". . . Naiche was wild and suspicious and evidently feared treachery. He knew that the once noted leader, Mangus-Colorado, had, years ago, been foully murdered after he had surrendered, and the last hereditary chief of the hostile Apaches hesitated to place himself in the hands of the pale-faces. . . ."

Continuing his report, General Howard says:

". . . I believed at first from official reports that the surrender was unconditional, except that the troops themselves would not kill the hostiles. Now, from General Miles's dispatches and from his annual report, forwarded on the 21st instant by mail, the conditions are plain: First, that the lives of all the Indians should be spared. Second, that they should be sent to Fort Marion, Florida, where their tribe, including their families, had already been ordered. . . ."

D. S. Stanley, Brigadier General, telegraphs from San Antonio, Texas, October 22, 1886, as follows:

". . . Geronimo and Naiche requested an interview with me when they first ascertained that they were to leave here, and in talking to them, I told them the exact disposition that was to be made of them. They regarded the separation of themselves from their families as a violation of the terms of their treaty of surrender, by which they had been guaranteed, in the most positive manner conceivable to their minds, that they should be united with their families at Fort Marion.

"There were present at the talk they had with me Major J. P. Wright, surgeon, United States Army; Captain J. G. Balance, acting Judge-advocate, United States Army; George Wratton, the interpreter; Naiche, and Geronimo.[1]

"The Indians were separated from their families at this place; the women, children, and the two scouts were placed in a separate car before they left.

"In an interview with me they stated the following incident, which they regard as an essential part of their treaty of surrender, and which took place at Skeleton Cañon before they had, as a band, made up their minds to surrender, and before any of them, except perhaps Geronimo, had given up their arms, and when they were still fully able to escape and defend themselves.

"General Miles said to them: 'You go with me to Fort Bowie and at a certain time you will go to see your relatives in Florida.' After they went to Fort Bowie he reassured them that they would see their relatives in Florida in four and a half or five days.

"While at Skeleton Cañon General Miles said to them: 'I have come to have a talk with you.' The conversation was interpreted from English into Spanish and from Spanish into Apache and *vice versa*. The interpreting from English into Spanish was done by a man by the name of Nelson. The interpreting from Spanish into Apache was done by José Maria Yaskes. José Maria Montoya was also present, but he did not do any of the interpreting.

[1] Mr. George Wratton is now at Fort Sill, Oklahoma, acting as Superintendent of Apaches. He has been with the Apaches as interpreter and superintendent since their surrender. (SMB)

"Dr. Wood, United States Army, and Lieutenant Clay, Tenth Infantry, were present.[2]

"General Miles drew a line on the ground and said, 'This represents the ocean,' and, putting a small rock beside the line, he said, 'This represents the place where Chihuahua is with his band.' He then picked up another stone and placed it a short distance from the first, and said, 'This represents you, Geronimo.' He then picked up a third stone and placed it a little distance from the others, and said, 'This represents the Indians at Camp Apache. The President wants to take you and put you with Chihuahua.' He then picked up the stone which represented Geronimo and his band and put it beside the one which represented Chihuahua at Fort Marion. After doing this he picked up the stone which represented the Indians at Camp Apache and placed it beside the other two stones which represented Geronimo and Chihuahua at Fort Marion, and said, 'That is what the President wants to do, get all of you together.'

"After their arrival at Fort Bowie General Miles said to them, 'From now on we want to begin a new life,' and holding up one of his hands with the palm open and horizontal he marked lines across it with the finger of the other hand and said, pointing to his open palm, 'This represents the past; it is all covered with hollows and ridges,' then, rubbing his other palm over it, he said, 'That represents the wiping out of the past, which will be considered smooth and forgotten.'

"The interpreter, Wratton, says that he was present and heard this conversation. The Indians say that Captain Thompson, Fourth Cavalry, was also present.

"Naiche said that Captain Thompson, who was the acting assistant adjutant general, Department of Arizona, told him at his house in Fort Bowie, 'Don't be afraid; no harm shall come

[2] Dr. Leonard Wood, later Army Chief of Staff. (FT)

to you. You will go to your friends all right.' He also told them 'that Fort Marion is not a very large place, and is not probably large enough for all, and that probably in six months or so you will be put in a larger place, where you can do better.' He told them the same thing when they took their departure in the cars from Fort Bowie.

"The idea that they had of the treaty of surrender given in this letter is forwarded at their desire, and, while not desiring to comment on the matter, I feel compelled to say that my knowledge of the Indian character, and the experience I have had with Indians of all kinds, and the corroborating circumstances and facts that have been brought to my notice in this particular case, convince me that the foregoing statement of Naiche and Geronimo is substantially correct."

Extract from the annual report (1886) of the Division of the Pacific, commanded by Major General O. O. Howard, U.S. Army.

"Headquarters Division of the Pacific,
"Presidio of San Francisco, Cal.
"September 17, 1886.

"ADJUTANT GENERAL,
"U.S. Army, Washington, D.C.:
"GENERAL: I have the honor to submit the following report upon military operations and the condition of the Division of the Pacific for the information of the Lieutenant General, and to make some suggestions for his consideration:

.   .   .

"On the 17th of May, 1885, a party of about fifty of the Chiricahua prisoners, headed by Geronimo, Naiche, and other chiefs, escaped from the White Mountain Reserve, in Arizona, and entered upon a career of murder and robbery unparalleled in the history of Indian raids.

"Since then, and up to the time of my assuming command of this division, they had been pursued by troops with varying success.

"After the assassination of Captain Crawford, on January 11, by the Mexicans, the hostiles asked for a 'talk,' and finally had a conference on March 25, 26, and 27, with General Crook, in the Cañon of Los Embudos, 25 miles south of San Bernardino, Mexico, on which latter date it was arranged that they should be conducted by Lieutenant Manus, with his battalion of scouts, to Fort Bowie, Ariz.

"The march commenced on the morning of March 28 and proceeded until the night of the 29th, when, becoming excited with fears of possible punishment, Geronimo and Naiche, with twenty men, fourteen women, and two boys, stampeded to the hills. Lieutenant Manus immediately pursued, but without success.

.　　.　　.

"Simultaneously with my taking command of the division Brigadier General Crook was relieved by Brigadier General Miles, who at once set out to complete the task commenced by his predecessor.

"Geronimo and his band were committing depredations, now in the United States and now in Mexico, and, being separated into small parties, easily eluded the troops, and carried on their work of murder and outrage.

"Early in May General Miles organized the hostile field of operations into districts, each with its command of troops, with specific instructions to guard the water holes, to cover the entire ground by scouting parties, and give the hostiles no rest.

"An effective command, under Captain Lawton, Fourth Cavalry, was organized for a long pursuit.

"On May 3 Captain Lebo, Tenth Cavalry, had a fight with Geronimo's band 12 miles southwest of Santa Cruz, in Mexico, with a loss of one soldier killed and one wounded. After this fight the Indians retreated southward followed by three troops of cavalry.

"On May 12 a serious fight of Mexican troops with the hostiles near Planchos, Mexico, resulted in a partial defeat of the Mexicans.

"On May 15 Captain Hatfield's command engaged Geronimo's band in the Corrona Mountains, suffering a loss of two killed and three wounded, and the loss of several horses and mules, the Indians losing several killed.

"On May 16 Lieutenant Brown, Fourth Cavalry, struck the hostiles near Buena Vista, Mexico, capturing several horses, rifles, and a quantity of ammunition.

"The usual series of outrages, with fatiguing chase by troops, continued until June 21, when the Mexicans engaged the hostiles about 40 miles southeast of Magdalena, Mexico, and after a stubborn fight repulsed them. . . .

.   .   .

"About the middle of August Geronimo and his band were so reduced and harassed by the tireless pursuit of the soldiers that they made offer of surrender to the Mexicans, but without coming to terms.

"Their locality thus being definitely known, disposition of the troops was rapidly made to act in conjunction with the Mexicans to intercept Geronimo and force his surrender.

"On August 25 Geronimo, when near Fronteraz, Mexico,

recognizing that he was pretty well surrounded, and being out of ammunition and food, made overtures of capitulation, through Lieutenant Gatewood, Sixth Cavalry, to Captain Lawton. He desired certain terms, but was informed that a surrender as prisoner of war was all that would be accepted.

"The Indians then proceeded to the vicinity of Captain Lawton's command, near Skeleton Cañon, and sent word that they wished to see General Miles.

"On September 3 General Miles arrived at Lawton's camp, and on September 4 Naiche, the son of Cochise, and the hereditary chief of the Apaches, with Geronimo surrendered all the hostiles, with the understanding, it seems, that they should be sent out of Arizona.

"I am not informed of the exact nature of this surrender, at first deemed unconditional. . . .

.   .   .

"I am, sir, very respectfully, your obedient servant,
"O. O. HOWARD,
"Major General, United States Army."

STATEMENT OF W. T. MELTON,
ANADARKO, OKLAHOMA

From 1882 to 1887 I lived in southern Arizona, and was employed by the Sansimone Cattle Company.

In 1886 I was stationed in Skeleton Cañon, about 10 miles north of the boundary line between Arizona and Old Mexico, with J. D. Prewitt. It was our duty to ride the lines south of our range and keep the cattle of the Company from straying into Old Mexico.

One afternoon, when returning from our ride, we discovered an Indian trail leading toward our camp. We rode hurriedly out of the hills into a broad valley so that we could better discover any attacking parties of Apaches and if assailed have at least a fighting chance for our lives. We knew the Apaches under Geronimo were on the warpath, but they were far down in Old Mexico. However, our knowledge of the Indians led us to expect anything at any time—to always be ready for the worst.

When we reached the valley we struck a cavalry trail also headed for our camp. This was perplexing, for neither the Indians nor the soldiers seemed to have been riding fast, and both trails led toward our camp in Skeleton Cañon. This cañon was a natural route from Old Mexico to Arizona, and almost all bands of Indians, as well as detachments of United States troops, passed and repassed through this valley when going to Old Mexico or returning therefrom, but never before had two hostile bands passed through here at the same time and traveling in the same direction, except when one fled and the other pursued. What this could mean was a mystery to us. Could it be that the troops had not seen the Indians? Were the redskins trying to head the troops off and attack them in their camp? Were the troops hunting for those Indians? Could this be Lawton's command? Could that be Geronimo's band? No, it was impossible. Then who were these troops and what Indians were those?

Cautiously we rode to our camp, and nailed on the door of our cabin was this notice:

"BE CAREFUL, GERONIMO IS NEAR BY AND HAS NOT YET SURRENDERED.

"CAPT. LAWTON."

Then we understood.

A short distance above our cabin we found the camp of the troops and we had just finished talking with Captain Law-

182

ton, who advised us to remain in his camp rather than risk staying alone in our cabin, when up rode the chief, Geronimo. He was mounted on a blaze-faced, white-stockinged dun horse.

He came directly to Captain Lawton and through an interpreter asked who we were and what we wanted.

As soon as the explanation was given he nodded his approval and rode away.

Prewitt and I rode away with him. We were well armed and well mounted and Geronimo was well mounted, but so far as we could see unarmed. I tried to talk with the chief (in English), but could not make him understand. Prewitt wanted to shoot him and said he could easily kill him the first shot, but I objected and succeeded in restraining him.[3] While we were arguing the chief rode silently between us, evidently feeling perfectly secure. All this time we had been riding in the direction of our horses that were grazing in the valley about a mile distant from our corral. When we came to a place about a half mile from Lawton's camp, where a spur of the mountain ran far out into the valley, Geronimo turned aside, saluted, said in fairly good Spanish, *"Adios, Señors,"* and began to ascend a mountain path. Later we learned that he was going directly toward his camp far up among the rocks. We rode on, drove our horses back to the corral and remained in our cabin all night, but were not molested by the Indians.

The next day we killed three beeves for the Indians, and they were paid for by Captain Lawton. On the second day two mounted Mexican scouts came to Lawton's camp. As

[3] Recently Mr. Melton told Geronimo of this conversation. The wily old chief laughed slyly and said, "What if Prewitt's pistol had been knocked out of his hand? Other men have tried to shoot me and at least some of them failed. But I'm glad he didn't try it." (SMB)

A C. S. Fly photograph of the hostiles' camp at Cañon de los Embudos during the negotiations with General Crook. (COURTESY OF FORT SILL MUSEUM, FORT SILL, OKLAHOMA)

soon as these Mexicans came in sight the Indians seized their arms and vanished, as it were, among the rocks.

Captain Lawton wrote an account of conditions and delivered it to the Mexicans, who withdrew. After they had gone and their mission had been explained to Geronimo the Indians again returned to their camp and laid down their arms.

On the next day word reached camp that General Miles was approaching and the Indians again armed and disappeared among the rocks. (Many of the Apache squaws had field glasses and were stationed every day on prominent mountain peaks to keep a lookout.[4] No one could approach their camp or Lawton's camp without being discovered by these spies.)

Soon after General Miles joined Lawton's command Geronimo rode into camp unarmed, and dismounting approached General Miles, shook hands with him, and then stood proudly before the officers waiting for General Miles to begin conversation with him.

The interpreter said to Geronimo, "General Miles is your friend." Geronimo said, "I never saw him, but I have been in need of friends. Why has he not been with me?" When this answer was interpreted everybody laughed. After this there was no more formality and without delay the discussion of the treaty was begun. All I remember distinctly of the treaty is that Geronimo and his band were not to be killed, but they were to be taken to their families.

I remember this more distinctly, because the Indians were so much pleased with this particular one of the terms of the treaty.

Geronimo, Naiche, and a few others went on ahead with

---

[4] These field glasses were taken from soldiers and officers (Mexicans and Americans) whom the Apaches had killed. (SMB)

General Miles, but the main band of Indians left under the escort of Lawton's troops.

The night before they left, a young squaw, daughter-in-law of Geronimo, gave birth to a child. The next morning the husband, Geronimo's son, carried the child, but the mother mounted her pony unaided and rode away unassisted—a prisoner of war under military escort.

On the afternoon of the day of the treaty Captain Lawton built a monument (about ten feet across and six feet high) of rough stones at the spot where the treaty was made. The next year some cowboys on a round-up camped at the place, and tore down the monument to see what was in it. All they found was a bottle containing a piece of paper upon which was written the names of the officers who were with Lawton.

After the Indians left we found one hundred and fifty dollars and twenty-five cents ($150.25) in Mexican money hidden in a rat's nest near where the Indians had camped.[5]

About ten o'clock on the morning after the Apaches and soldiers had gone away twenty Pimos Indians, accompanied by one white man, surrounded our camp and demanded to know of Geronimo's whereabouts. We told them of the treaty and they followed the trail on toward Fort Bowie.

That afternoon, thinking all danger from Apaches past, my partner, Prewitt, went to ride the lines and I was left in camp alone. I was pumping water (by horse-power) at the well, when I saw three Indians rounding up our horses about half a mile away. They saw me but did not disturb me, nor did I interfere with them, but as soon as they had driven that bunch of horses northward over the hill out of sight I rode quickly off in another direction and drove another bunch of horses

[5] This was a stick nest built on top of the ground by a species of woods rat. (SMB)

Geronimo. From a photograph by DeLancey Gill, 1905. *(COURTESY OF THE SMITHSONIAN INSTITUTION: NATIONAL ANTHROPOLOGICAL ARCHIVES)*

into the corral. The rest of the afternoon I stayed in camp, but saw no more Indians.

The next day we rode over the hill in the direction these Indians had gone and found that they had camped not three miles away. There were evidently several in the party and they had kept scouts concealed near the top of the hill to watch me, and to shoot me from ambush had I followed them. This we knew because we saw behind some rocks at the crest of the hill in the loose soil the imprints left by the bodies of three warriors where they had been lying down in concealment.

At their camp we found the head and hoofs of my favorite horse, "Digger," a fine little sorrel pony, and knew that he had served them for dinner. We followed their trail far into Old Mexico, but did not overtake them. We had been accustomed to say "it was Geronimo's band," whenever any depredation was committed, but this time we were not so positive.

.   .   .

We do not wish to express our own opinion, but to ask the reader whether, after having had the testimony of Apaches, soldiers, and civilians, who knew the conditions of surrender, and, after having examined carefully the testimony offered, it would be possible to conclude that Geronimo made an unconditional surrender?

Before passing from this subject it would be well also to consider whether our Government has treated these prisoners in strict accordance with the terms of the treaty made in Skeleton Cañon.

A Selected Bibliography

Andrist, Ralph K. *The Long Death: The Last Days of the Plains Indians.* New York: Macmillan, 1964; Collier Books, 1969.

Clum, Woodworth. *Apache Agent: The Story of John P. Clum.* Boston: Houghton-Mifflin, 1936.

Davis, Britton. *The Truth about Geronimo.* New Haven: Yale University Press, 1929.

Debo, Angie. *Geronimo: The Man, His Time, His Place.* Norman: University of Oklahoma Press, 1976.

Drinnon, Richard. *Facing West: The Metaphysics of Indian-Hating and Empire-Building.* Minneapolis: University of Minnesota Press, 1980; New York: Schocken Books, 1990.

Farb, Peter. *Man's Rise to Civilization as Shown by the Indians of North America from Primeval Times to the Coming of the Industrial State.* New York: E. P. Dutton, 1968; second edition, 1978.

Faulk Odie, B. *The Geronimo Campaign.* New York: Oxford University Press, 1969.

Goodwin, Grenville. *The Social Organization of the Western Apache.* Chicago: University of Chicago Press, 1942.

Lockwood, Frank C. *The Apache Indians*. New York: Macmillan, 1938.

Matthiessen, Peter. *In the Spirit of Crazy Horse*. New York: Viking Press, 1983; second edition, Viking Penguin, 1991.

Opler, Morris E. *An Apache Life-Way*. Chicago: University of Chicago Press, 1941.

————. *Myths and Tales of the Chiricahua Apache Indians*. Philadelphia: American Folk-Lore Society, 1942; Lincoln: University of Nebraska Press, 1994.

Roberts, David. *Once They Moved like the Wind: Cochise, Geronimo, and the Apache Wars*. New York: Simon & Schuster, 1993, 1994.

Schellie, Don. *Vast Domain of Blood: The Story of the Camp Grant Massacre*. Los Angeles: Westernlore, 1968.

Thrapp, Dan L. *The Conquest of Apacheria*. Norman: University of Oklahoma Press, 1967.

Worcester, Donald E. *The Apaches: Eagles of the Southwest*. Norman: University of Oklahoma Press, 1979, 1992.